T0318501

Cambridge Elements ☰

Elements in Applied Linguistics
edited by
Li Wei
University College London
Zhu Hua
University College London

NEW FRONTIERS
IN LANGUAGE
AND TECHNOLOGY

Christopher Joseph Jenks
Utrecht University

CAMBRIDGE
UNIVERSITY PRESS

Shaftesbury Road, Cambridge CB2 8EA, United Kingdom

One Liberty Plaza, 20th Floor, New York, NY 10006, USA

477 Williamstown Road, Port Melbourne, VIC 3207, Australia

314–321, 3rd Floor, Plot 3, Splendor Forum, Jasola District Centre, New Delhi – 110025, India

103 Penang Road, #05–06/07, Visioncrest Commercial, Singapore 238467

Cambridge University Press is part of Cambridge University Press & Assessment, a department of the University of Cambridge.

We share the University's mission to contribute to society through the pursuit of education, learning and research at the highest international levels of excellence.

www.cambridge.org
Information on this title: www.cambridge.org/9781009184397

DOI: 10.1017/9781009184403

First published 2023

A catalogue record for this publication is available from the British Library.

ISBN 978-1-009-18439-7 Paperback
ISSN 2633-5069 (online)
ISSN 2633-5050 (print)

New Frontiers in Language and Technology

Elements in Applied Linguistics

DOI: 10.1017/9781009184403
First published online: June 2023

Christopher Joseph Jenks
Utrecht University
Author for correspondence: Christopher Joseph Jenks, c.j.jenks@uu.nl

Abstract: The Fourth Industrial Revolution (4IR) describes the technological transformations that are incrementally, but radically, changing everyday life practices. Like previous industrial revolutions, technological advancements are so pervasive and impactful that everything from an individual's sense of identity and understanding of the world to the economic success of an entire industry are profoundly altered by 4IR innovation. Despite the significance of 4IR transformations, little applied linguistic research has examined how these emergent technologies collectively transform human behavior and communication. To this end, this Element identifies key 4IR issues and outlines how they relate to applied linguistic research. The Element argues that applied linguists are in an excellent position to contribute to such research, as expertise in language and communication is critical to understanding 4IR issues. However, to make interdisciplinary and wider societal contributions, applied linguists must rethink how 4IR technologies can be harnessed to more efficiently publish and disseminate timely research.

Keywords: technology, computer-mediated communication, human-machine interface, human-computer interaction, automation

ISBNs: 9781009184397 (PB), 9781009184403 (OC)
ISSNs: 2633-5069 (online), 2633-5050 (print)

Contents

1 The 4th Industrial Revolution: An Introduction   1

2 The Human-Machine Interface: Emergent Technologies
in Everyday Life   11

3 Digital Economies: From Gig Work to Cryptocurrencies   21

4 Communicating Threats: Security Breaches, Language
Injustices, Civil Subjugation, and Other Dangers   30

5 Systems of Power: Regulating Information
and Communication   38

6 Conclusion: The Role of Applied Linguistics   45

References   58

1 The 4th Industrial Revolution: An Introduction

It's the usual utopian vision. This time they were saying it'll reduce waste. If stores know what their customers want, then they don't overproduce, don't overship, don't have to throw stuff away when it's not bought. I mean, like everything else you guys are pushing, it sounds perfect, sounds progressive, but it carries with it more control, more central tracking of everything we do.

—Dave Eggers, The Circle

The delicate partnership that exists between sharing and protecting sensitive information is explored in *The Circle*, a dystopian story of the perils of technological advancement and global digitalization. Dave Eggers invites readers to consider what it means to advance in a society increasingly dependent on a network of personal information, underlining the precarious state of being married to the life conveniences afforded to us by technology. The story follows an employee that ostensibly benefits from working at a Big Tech company, though the reader is ultimately presented with a dark picture of how basic human experiences and practices are mediated by powerful institutions.

Although this Element on new frontiers in language and technology does not present the same dark picture, there are many aspects of life that are radically changing because of technological advancement and digital reliance yet remain under the empirical radar for most applied linguists. This gap in understanding must be narrowed, as technology advances at a rate far greater than the time it takes to conduct, disseminate, and publish relevant studies. As a result, there is a real danger in not knowing how technology is presently shaping many aspects of life, as well as what lies ahead for humans in a world progressively anchored to digital spaces. A key example of this danger is ChatGPT, which has generated much hysteria and conjecture within and outside of academia, yet its technological features and social consequences remain largely unknown.

A necessary first step in addressing related concerns is to name the technological and social changes occurring around us, as doing so will help direct attention to the collective transformations and transitions taking place because of technology and digitalization. To this end, many writers and scholars agree that we are currently living in a momentous time in which societies are experiencing revolutionary changes in how human behavior and communication are mediated by technology and digitalization, yet there are many competing terms used in academia and mainstream media. "Digital Age," "Information Age," and "Industry 4.0" are some of the more common terms used in writing. Such terms provide a macro lens through which to understand ongoing technological and social changes, but they all fail to signal the historical significance, as well as technological importance, of emerging technologies and digital spaces.

Conversely, the Fourth Industrial Revolution (4IR) is a term that reminds us that radical transformations have occurred in the past, as was the case with, for instance, the lifestyle changes that developed because of assembly-line technology during the Second Industrial Revolution. As a terminological construct, 4IR places ongoing technological transformations within a long history of profoundly impactful moments in time. These revolutionary eras are best understood by looking at the many "things" in life that are being transformed because of technology.

To this end, this Element identifies what these 4IR "things" are and why they matter for applied linguists. Presenting an overview of how applied linguists can investigate new frontiers in language and technology – and thus championing the cause for further research in related empirical areas – requires taking a somewhat neutral position with regard to epistemology, theory, and methodology. To this end, it is sensible to begin this Element by establishing a few important definitions.

Klaus Schwab (2018, p. 7), founder of the World Economic Forum, offers a useful starting point for the present discussion in his definition of 4IR.

The Fourth Industrial Revolution is a way of describing a set of ongoing and impending transformations in the systems that surround us, and which most of us take for granted every day. While it may not feel momentous to those of us experiencing a series of small but significant adjustments to daily life, it is not a minor change—the Fourth Industrial Revolution is a new chapter in human development, on par with the first, second and third Industrial Revolutions, and once again driven by the increasing availability and interaction of a set of extraordinary technologies.

According to this definition, 4IR is no different than previous revolutions: Societies are embedded within – that is, they are inextricably connected to – a system of technologies. As such, societies will, at different points in time, experience revolutionary changes because of technological advancements.

However, what are these "things" that are currently revolutionizing how life is understood and conducted? Answering this question involves first locating the fundamental difference in today's current revolutionary changes: 4IR technologies marry two domains of life that were once thought to have existed in separate dimensions: the physical world and the digital world. Here, the term phygital is a useful reference point in discussions of 4IR technologies and their far-reaching and transformative capabilities.

Phygital: The term combines the words physical and digital to denote the experiences derived from the marriage between material and electronic spaces. Phygital is not a term that is widely used in applied linguistic scholarship, though there are several notable studies that examine the communicative features of people simultaneously attending to physical and digital spaces (Due & Toft, 2021).

Phygital examples include augmented reality (AR), artificial intelligence (AI), and virtual reality (VR). These terms should be familiar to most readers, though it is nonetheless useful to establish definitions for them.

AI: Artificial intelligence refers to machines, including software programs and systems, that perform intelligent tasks that humans cannot do or do less efficiently. AI machines can often learn to perform more effectively or efficiently over time by gathering and managing information that they process. References to AI within the applied linguistic literature are often limited to brief, macro-level discussions of such technologies. That is, few applied linguistic studies investigate how AI mediates human language and communication, though there are a small number of notable exceptions (e.g., Dodigovic, 2005).

VR: Virtual reality is a digital 3D environment created using machines for humans to experience. VR relies on hardware devices in the physical world, such as goggles and gloves, to create immersive and interactive environments. While VR is a term that is taken up empirically by few applied linguists, the technology is much more commercial and mainstream than AI. Nevertheless, there are very few publications on VR in comparison to other technologies studied in applied linguistic research (for a recent discussion of the potential of VR in language learning, see Andujar & Buchner, 2019).

AR: Augmented reality is the physical world sensorily enhanced through the use of machines, such as picture-taking filters that alter the looks of humans, glasses that process information, such as foreign languages, digital maps that are used on phones as users navigate directions, or even chopsticks that enhance the flavors of foods. AR is a relatively new term in mainstream society, and applied linguistic research has not investigated this technology in any systematic way. AR has the potential to transform how students learn languages, such as using technology to enhance sensations while learning in digital spaces.

AI, VR, and AR are not cutting-edge examples of technology. However, such technologies are embedded into, or essential to, many aspects of life, such as searching for the best deals, finding life partners, participating in communities, marketing products, and curating information for individual needs. Thus, 4IR must not only be discussed as a set of individual technologies, but also as a way of life (e.g., the gig economy, biomedicine, and cybersecurity).

Although there is general agreement on the significance of technological advancement and global digitalization, scholars have different ways of characterizing what societies are currently experiencing with regard to technology. Indeed, there is general disagreement regarding the timing of 4IR with some critics even suggesting that we are still currently in the Third Industrial Revolution (3IR). This third era of revolutionary change started over five decades ago with the emerging use of what would now be characterized as primitive automation and up to, and even possibly beyond, the early years of the Internet and the widespread use of portable telecommunication devices.

Many of the defining technologies of 3IR are still in use in some form today, such as AI tools and robotic technology, leading many scholars to question whether societies are in fact in a fourth period of revolutionary change. For example, the personal computers and advanced telecommunication tools of the 1990s are key artifacts of 3IR, but have sufficient radical changes occurred subsequently to qualify a transition into 4IR? This issue of whether societies are currently in 3IR or 4IR is important to appreciate how technologies are embedded within everyday life practices at unprecedented levels of control and ubiquity. For instance, many current and emerging transformations evolved from 3IR technologies. However, there are new transformational characteristics of today's technologies, such as technology's ability to rapidly and seamlessly embed itself into many domains of life with significant consequences for both ordinary individuals and powerful institutions.

In other words, current technologies influence more societies and with greater complexity than ever before. Identifying what this influence entails will help establish why societies are currently experiencing 4IR transformations. To this end, there are three characteristics of technological transformations that distinguish life as we presently know it: system impact; breadth and depth; and velocity. According to Schwab (2017, p. 3), these three characteristics that he identifies in this book also support the argument that current technologies are 4IR in nature, as illustrated in Figure 1.

The impetus for writing this Element lies in these three characteristics: Technological advancement and global digitalization are transforming life at rapid pace and considerable reach. However, system impact, velocity, and breadth and depth make it difficult to keep track of the extent to which technology and digitalization are shaping life as we presently know it, as well as what lies ahead in the future as technological transformations become more deeply embedded within societies. What we know is that there are incremental, yet continuous, transformations in nearly all aspects of life, such as communication, transportation, and media consumption. Our evolving abilities to communicate with people from geographically displaced regions, the technological

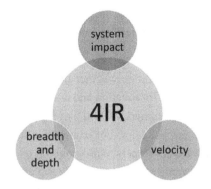

Figure 1 4IR technological transformation

1. **Velocity**: Current transformations are "evolving at an exponential rather than linear pace" because "new technology begets newer and ever more capable technology" (Schwab, 2017, p. 3)
2. **Breadth and depth**: Current transformations expand "on the digital revolution" and are based on "technologies that are leading to unprecedented paradigm shifts." (Schwab, 2017, p. 3)
3. **Systems impact**: Current transformations are embedded in "entire systems, across (and within) countries, companies, industries and society as a whole." (Schwab, 2017, p. 3)

advancements that push the ways in which it is possible to travel, and insatiable desires to always be connected or online alter how we understand once basic and static concepts, such as time, space, memory, and truth.

It is now necessary to, as a field of study, take stock of emerging technologies and catalog how language is anchored to ongoing transformations. To this end, what are the key technologies that define 4IR?

As identified earlier, a central 4IR feature is the marriage between physical objects and digital spaces. Wearable devices that monitor heart beats, biometric scanners in buildings, and appliances capable of doing basic home tasks through smart phones are just a few of the many phygital examples transforming how life is managed and understood. A useful term for describing such examples is the "Internet of Things."

Internet of Things: Things in the material world that are embedded with, or connected to, digital capabilities, applications, or systems. One of the most potentially impactful examples of our connection to the digital world is the metaverse.

Metaverse: The next generation of the Internet that combines VR and AR to provide users with immersive and interactive spaces – many readers will know of Second Life, which is an earlier form of a metaverse space that allows users to live life in an alternative world. The metaverse is an ambitious project by institutions to transform the Internet from something that you see to something that you are in.

While it is too early to determine whether the metaverse will become the primary way individuals share information and interact online, it is clear that an Internet that is completely immersive will have profound implications for human communication and behavior. For example, a fully operational metaverse will compel software developers to program VR and AR capabilities into existing communication applications, resulting in avatars replacing texts, emojis, and even keyboards. Such changes are already taking place: Facebook, for instance, recently changed its organizational name to Meta to reflect the company's desire to transition into, and possibly control, the metaverse.

The metaverse is a stark and unsettling example of digitalization following a steep upward trajectory of evolution. Despite the importance of digitization, 4IR transformations are materializing in domains of life beyond the physical and digital, and are not limited to accessing information on the Internet and communicating on social media platforms. For instance, Meta is currently working on an AI-powered "universal speech translator" capable of translations and interpretations in most world languages. This device, if created, would pose a number of societal and empirical issues that governments and researchers must address, such as the likelihood of such technologies exacerbating or solving existing power dynamics within and across world and marginalized languages (Vincent, 2022).

Technological advancements in biology are also driving 4IR forward, creating opportunities to better understand, and improve the health of, the human body. For instance, the identification and treatment of diseases through genetic sequencing and editing offer uncharted possibilities for healthcare providers. However, a host of social dilemmas and ethical challenges are tied to such possibilities. One such possibility includes the ability to cure life-threatening diseases through stem cell treatments and the ways in which biotechnologies will alter how societies view the human biology and acceptable forms of research.

Machines and robots are additionally central to discussions of 4IR, biology, and healthcare. Efforts to cut costs, provide more efficient medical treatment, and fill the shortage of health professionals have led many hospitals to turn to machines and robots for anything from mundane tasks, such as delivering medicine to patients, to complex responsibilities, such as diagnosing diseases and illnesses. In an exceptional case of technology merging with medical services, prototypes of robotic nurses are being created to explore the boundaries of technological innovation in healthcare. In June of 2021, for instance, Reuters circulated a story of a trilingual Cantonese-Mandarin-English robot nurse that was created to not only resemble a human, but to also treat patients with empathetic facial expressions (Master, 2021). Although there is still a long way to go before robotic nurses will replace humans at any notable scale, this example offers a glimpse into what the future holds for societies.

Similarly, text-based chat tools exploit AI technologies to provide unrestricted time access to advice for individuals with questions or concerns about their health outside of normal office hours. In other similar communicative contexts, traditional digital communication tools, such as video calls, are being used by medical doctors to provide advice to patients living in remote or geographically displaced areas. Both examples of telemedicine offer a window into how technology blurs the boundary between time and space.

In other contexts, technological advancements in manufacturing, and more specifically 3D printing, are being used to transform biology. A notable example includes fabricating human body parts and tissues using 3D technologies, which is a process referred to as biofabrication.

Biofabrication: The "rapid construction of 3D structures with complex geometries using a diverse range of synthetic and natural materials. Recent breakthroughs have enabled 3D printing of cells, biocompatible materials, and supporting components into complex 3D functional living tissues." (Atala & Yoo, 2015 p. xvii).

Biofabrication is an emerging area of interdisciplinary study with its own journal and professional organization. The legal discourse and ethical standards that prop up the study and application of biofabrication are two of many areas of research to which applied linguists can contribute. In other interdisciplinary research, the discursive construction and dissemination of biofabrication in popular culture, such as the texts and images of humanoids and cyborgs found in movies and novels, offer cutting-edge opportunities for applied linguists to work with literary and media scholars to make sense of how 4IR technologies distill past fictions into present realities. All examples of interdisciplinary research into biofabrication feed into a greater understanding of the ways in which 4IR technologies and transformations shape the path from which society takes.

This brief overview of 4IR thus far establishes the ways in which revolutionary technologies are consequential to many aspects of life from mundane communication to life-changing medical procedures. The significance of 4IR was discussed in this section in relation to three aspects of life, or what Schwab (2016, p. 14) refers to as megatrends: physical, digital, and biological.

Megatrends represent clusters of technologies that are both pervasive and impactful. However, each cluster indexes a range of language and communication issues that are central to understanding 4IR transformation, which Schwab (2016) does not attend to in his seminal book.

Before presenting how subsequent sections are organized to address specific issues related to language, communication, and technology, it is necessary to briefly outline the reasons why applied linguists should care about, and conduct research on, 4IR issues. To this end, the first step in outlining why applied linguists should care about language and technology is to return to a definition of the discipline in which this Element is situated. That is, applied linguists are primarily interested in the study of "real-world problems in which language is a central issue" (Brumfit, 1995, p. 27). Although applied linguistic research spans a range of empirical issues related to real-world problems, there are three social processes that are integral to an understanding of language and technology. As illustrated in Figure 2, these three social processes are mediation, system, and order.

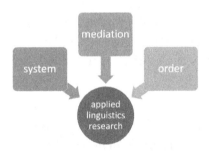

Figure 2 4IR and applied linguistic research

1. **Mediation**: Language is constantly in a state of flux, changing because of its users and adapting to the context in which communication occurs. Technology amplifies these processes by creating new modes of, and tools for, communication. Similarly, existing language structures and communicative practices mediate the ways in which technology is conceived and put into practice. 4IR brings technology and language closer together by further blurring the boundaries between physical and digital spaces while accelerating the speed in which this fusion occurs.

2. **System**: Digital technologies are systems of social practice that influence, if not dictate, how we do basic human tasks, such as relying on social media to communicate with friends and completing government forms using online

Caption for Figure 2 (cont.)

platforms. 4IR technologies are used for existing societal functions and therefore embedded within institutions (e.g., using machines for assembly line production); but they can also function as systems with their own communicative or social purpose (e.g., wearable devices that monitor health information). Although humans are responsible for creating digital systems, technology can ultimately govern our behaviors, communication, and ideologies. Digital economies, for example, rely heavily on AI technologies that curate information so that consumers feel, think, and ultimately make decisions, in a particular or even predefined way.

3. **Order**: 4IR technologies can be used by states and institutions to create, maintain, or even disrupt order in societies. Establishing an ideal code of conduct within society, determining what is right and wrong from a legal standpoint, and predicting future criminal behavior are examples of how 4IR technologies are being used, and can be implemented in the future, to establish order within and across states and institutions. For instance, 4IR technologies can be used to process millions of biometric files to search for criminals or establish criteria that predict whether an individual will likely commit a crime in the future.

Mediation, system, and order are not new social processes. All three examples influencing how we interact, behave, and think can be found throughout human history. 4IR technologies are unique, however, in terms of magnitude, scope, and velocity, as discussed earlier in this section.

Furthermore, 4IR is particularly unique in the moral dualism that comes with how emerging technologies are used for the "greater good" of society. Many of the life conveniences that we enjoy in society, such as "free" and "tailored" online services, come at a cost (e.g., privacy and security). The ideologies and language used to think about and communicate what privacy and security mean in a world driven by technology are topics that are primed for important future applied linguistic research, as discussed in subsequent sections.

To this end, the contents of this Element are devoted to introducing several 4IR topics that represent both urgent and exciting research opportunities in the study of language and technology. Of course, with all books, it is necessary to provide an obligatory caveat before moving forward: The empirical topics and practical issues identified and discussed in subsequent sections are not comprehensive, but the contents of this Element do provide a sufficiently diverse and broad understanding of social transformations to offer a rich introductory account of new frontiers in language and technology while championing the study of 4IR technologies.

Section 2 explores the human-machine interface, identifying several emergent technologies and 4IR topics that are important to how language is organized and used in everyday life. The section is based largely on a discussion of biology and technology, and how these two facets of life are shaping human behavior and communication. Example topics include genetic manipulation, bioprinting, neurotechnology, and automated reasoning, which is a subfield of AI. Specific transformations and applications discussed in this section include brain chip companies, such as Neuralink Corporation, and the impact COVID-19 is currently having on social practices, such as how individuals think and feel about technology being used to confront global pandemics.

Section 3 moves into a more specific discussion of the economy, looking at how technological transformations change the discourses of money, business transactions, service providers, and work, to name a few. Example topics include the ways in which the gig economy is transforming the structure of human encounters, blockchain technology and its impact on government power, and the use of digital tools to create more sustainable economies. The section introduces topics that applied linguists can investigate, such as the use of profit-generating digital tools that prop up language and racial inequalities.

Section 4 addresses some of the more explicit problems associated with technological transformations and digital reliance. The section explores the real and potential dangers in relying on technology to carry out social practices from the mundane, such as using automated translation tools to decipher a website, to the complex, such as the role of institutions in censoring and canceling political figures. Example topics include the creation and dissemination of conspiracy theories on social media, the proliferation of fake news, troll farms and their role in political dissent, and language representation and diversity in online spaces.

Section 5 examines aspects of power in relation to 4IR in general, and the language-technology interface in particular. The section looks at what systems of power mean in a world driven by technology. For example, what are the power dynamics involved in using technology to create, disseminate, process, and understand sensitive, private, and public information? Can technology be trusted to make decisions that have a significant impact on the future of an individual, such as with mortgage, student loan, job, or immigration applications?

Section 6 concludes the discussion by exploring what it means to advance language and technology scholarship in world that is advancing at a rate much faster than the time needed to publish peer-reviewed empirical studies. The section examines old issues, such as the need to be more interdisciplinary, as well as newer ones, including reflecting on what it means to conduct ethical research in a digitalized world. Three key aspects of research are discussed in this section. The first aspect relates to the need to better utilize existing (and perhaps even emerging) technologies in applied linguistic research on language and technology. The second aspect is based on the urgency to conduct and disseminate research that reflects how societies use technologies to create and consume information. Relatedly, the third aspect deals with readership and audience; that is, how can applied linguistic scholarship reach a larger audience, and more specifically, readers that make policy and institutional decisions on how technologies are used?

Although new frontiers in language and technology are discussed as disparate issues presented in different sections, 4 IR transformations are entangled in a web of language and technology issues. Therefore, readers are encouraged to reflect on how one technology presented in a section may participate in the application of different technologies discussed in other sections.

2 The Human-Machine Interface: Emergent Technologies in Everyday Life

The human-machine interface refers to the relationship that humans have with machines, and the ways in which our partnership with technology influences how we think, communicate, and behave. This relationship with machines is becoming more intimate as societies advance, reflecting our increasing desires to employ technologies to assist, or even replace, how we manage daily life functions and tasks. Machines are present and influential in a range of life functions and tasks from the extraordinarily mundane, such as using a smart phone to change the lighting in a room, to the exceptionally complex, such as implanting chips in the human body. A discussion of machines must not be limited to hardware devices or mechanical systems, but should rather include the software technologies and developments that enable such "equipment" to function. A concrete example of this marriage between software and hardware is machine learning (ML).

ML is an area of study devoted to discovering how best to program machines, or more specifically computers, that improve their functions through exposure to data (i.e., experience). Examples of ML include speech recognition, predictive analytics, image recognition, and chatbot programs (e.g., ChatGPT).

From this definition of ML (for an extended discussion, see Jordan & Mitchell, 2015), it can be said that machines are algorithms, programming language, and computational statistics as much as they are physical objects. So, discussing the human-machine interface requires a consideration of the processes that are responsible for the "intelligence" that hides behind mechanical and computer devices.

The human-machine interface is of paramount concern for developing and developed societies, as technological advancements are creating new reasons and opportunities to use machines and even replace them with humans. This reliance on machines is not new. Older technologies, such as hearing aids, have been used for communication by humans for over a century. In a crude way, the amplification of sounds through hearing aids works in a similar way to newer technologies, such as the ML system that runs Google Translate. Both old and new technologies process language data into something that humans can use or from which they benefit.

In this sense, while the technological developments from older to newer machines are remarkable, the underlying application remains the same: Machines are tools for human communication. They are created for, and by, us. What this interface will transform into in the next two or three decades is open to debate, but it is clear nevertheless that machines are integral to many aspects of life from how societies function to the minute details of how language and communication are organized.

For example, although machines have for many decades mediated our ability to use language, a new mode of human communication has materialized as a result of 4IR technologies. That is, in addition to using machines to aid in human communication, they have now become capable interlocutors as a result of recent AI advancements. This is most evident in the widespread use of chatbots.

Understanding the significance of chatbots to human communication requires unpacking its underlying technology. That is, what is a bot?

Bot is an AI application created to carry out automated tasks, such as locating information using a search engine (web crawler bots) or offering phone support for a customer (chatbots). Bots can also be programmed to perform unethical, bad, or illegal tasks, such as spamming inboxes (malicious bots), posting contentious information on social media platforms (social bots), and downloading private or personal information (web scraping bots).

Remarkably, bots are responsible for more internet traffic than humans (Barracuda, 2021). In other words, bots are responsible for much of what is produced and consumed on the Internet. The control that bots have over the creation, dissemination, and mediation of information is a reminder that the human-machine interface is not simply an esoteric research topic restricted to tech-savvy scholars, but rather such technologies are foundational to the future of human communication. Recent and revolutionary examples of the significance of bots can be found in discussions of chatbots in general, and ChatGPT in particular.

ChatGPT is an AI-powered chatbot that has the ability to hold a conversation on a wide range of topics from complex academic disciplines, such as neuroscience, to more ostensibly trivial issues, including vegan, gluten-free muffin recipes. Much discussion is currently taking place with regard to the power and potential of ChatGPT (also GPT-3), as the chatbot is capable of being used in unethical ways, such as writing essays for students. The GPT part of the name stands for *generative pre-trained transformer*, which is a type of ML that falls within the category of *large language model*. The underlying intelligence in such models is the ability to process enormous amounts of language information, creating predictions or doing guess work based on given data. A somewhat primitive example of this computational process is predicting word collocations. More impressive computational examples include creating a thought-provoking poem or designing a cognitively challenging syllabus for a course on ancient Greek philosophy.

While the benefits and opportunities of ChatGPT and other similar AI-powered tools should be celebrated, there are real concerns regarding the misuse of such technologies. Disseminating misinformation and disinformation, creating false certifications, and again completing assignments with the help of machines, are just a few of the many concerns that people have of AI and chatbots. In response to these concerns, AI tools are being created to uncover instances of misuse. One such example is GPTZero.

GPTZero is an AI-powered tool that can help determine whether a piece of writing was done by a large language model, such as ChatGPT. GPTZero uses statistical computations to measure whether text inputted into its system is human- or AI-generated. Several anecdotal accounts of using GPTZero by technology writers suggest that the program requires a substantial amount of further development before it can accurately and clearly make such distinctions. This observation is, of course, an empirical question that applied linguists can address in future research on language and technology.

ChatGPT and GPTZero illustrate the possibilities and threats that exist when societies are embedded within the human-machine interface. In terms of empirical possibilities for applied linguistic research, the human-machine interface can be expressed as two overlapping modes of communication: communicating with machines and communicating to machines. These modes of communication are illustrated in Figure 3.

For both domains of investigation, an obvious area of contribution that applied linguists can make is within the study of mediation: Understanding

Figure 3 Human-machine communication

1. **Communicating with machines**: A key area of applied linguistic research within language and technology is the question of how humans communicate with machines. Old and new technologies used by humans to communicate with machines include, but are not limited to, telegraphs, telephones, pagers, computer keyboards, and mobile phones. Recent applications of communicating with machines are typically mediated through software programs, such as WhatsApp, Signal, Messenger, Skype, Teams, and Zoom. Some applied linguistic research has been conducted within this domain of investigation, though there are many technologies that have received little to no attention in the literature.

2. **Communicating to machines**: A key area of applied linguistic research within language and technology is the question of how humans communicate to machines. Technologies used by humans to communicate to machines include virtual assistants, such as Apple's Siri and Amazon's Alexa, as well as the many machines used in hospitals, airports, and hotels (see Bonarini, 2020). Older examples of communicating to machines date back to as early as the 1960s (e.g., ELIZA; Weizenbaum, 1966), though many of these technologies were not available to the general public and only studied within the field of human-computer interaction (HCI), which was at the time an esoteric field (e.g., Grudin & Jacques, 2019).

how customers adjust their language to a chat bot while filing a complaint is one of many possibilities within this area of study worth pursuing.

Relatedly, AI systems that are capable of conversing with humans draw from research on speech act theory, conversation analysis, discourse analysis, as well as other methodological approaches to which many applied linguists dedicate their work. Applied linguists are thus in a unique position to offer critical interdisciplinary work to scholars and professionals responsible for designing and understanding 4IR technologies. For example, applied linguists and HCI scholars have many common research interests that could form the foundation of interesting and cutting-edge studies on language and technology.

One way of understanding the research opportunities that exist in the interdisciplinary study of 4IR technologies is to divide the human-machine interface into four modes of communication: human-machine-human, human-machine, machine-human, machine-machine. These modes of communication are depicted in Figure 4.

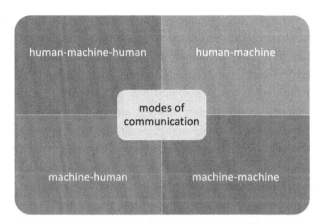

Figure 4 Human-machine modes of communication

1. **Human-machine-human**: Humans communicate with each other using hardware devices (e.g., keyboards, screens, microphones, headphones) and software programs (e.g., predictive texts, read receipts, speech-to-text software, and auto-fill scripts). Machines shape a number of linguistic features (e.g., conversational topic, style, turn-taking, word choice), but they do not often limit the breadth and depth of human communication. Like face-to-face exchanges, the topic of communication when mediated through machines can be anything from short and superficial to long and complex. The bulk of applied linguistic research on language and technology is devoted to understanding human-machine-human communication (e.g., examining how students communicate in the context of telecollaboration).

2. **Human-machine**: Humans can communicate to machines because AI technologies are designed to recognize speech and embodied actions (e.g., virtual assistants and robots). Machine are also programmed to process keywords, formulaic utterances, and scripted texts (e.g., chatbots). Accordingly, the type of communication that unfolds within this mode is typically short and superficial (e.g., limited to two-part exchanges or adjacency pairs), as most AI machines are preprogrammed to respond to a limited set of information. A clear exception to this observation is ChatGPT, which can generate essay-long responses on complex and varied topics. Technological advancements within human-machine communication are generating much discussion within and outside of academia, though applied linguistic research in this area is scarce.

Caption for Figure 4 (cont.)

3. **Machine-human**: Machines can also communicate to humans. This mode of communication often entails humans inputting information into AI systems for machines to communicate at a later date or time (e.g., task reminders, alarm clocks, location alerts, place directions, and fact changes). The content or topic of communication here may be complex (e.g., stock market fluctuations), but the exchange is often short and restricted to specific tasks, such as signaling to a family that their meatloaf is done. While machine-human communication has not attracted the attention of many applied linguists, there are several relevant empirical possibilities within this area of study, including examining how language is mediated when humans are prompted by machines to wrap up a task, such as an exercise in class assigned by a teacher.

4. **Machine-machine**: Machines communicate to machines in a number of ways that shape – behind the scenes – how humans manage and understand both mundane life tasks and professional work. For example, machines communicate to other machines when humans go online to check if particular goods are in stock, need to monitor home appliances from different locations, purchase services with digital wallets, or cross busy intersections by foot or car. Research opportunities are limited to contexts where machines produce some form of language to each other, such as when chatbots communicate with each other.

The role machines have in human communication is often taken for granted, as our handheld and computing devices are with us throughout the day on most occasions. However, understanding how to use, and becoming accustomed to the conveniences afforded to us by, such technologies does not mean that societies are in a better position to critically evaluate, or even appreciate, the profound influence machines have on human language and communication. Establishing a deeper understanding of the human-machine interface requires building a foundation of empirical knowledge for each mode of communication identified earlier.

To this end, the human-machine interface presents many empirical opportunities beyond the modes of communication identified previously. These overlapping empirical opportunities are (1) language, (2) communication, (3) human behavior, (4) spaces and places, (5) ideologies, (6) language learning, and (7) society. While not an exhaustive list of research possibilities, the seven empirical categories together offer a glimpse into how the human-machine interface is relevant to applied linguistic scholarship. These seven empirical categories are presented in Figure 5.

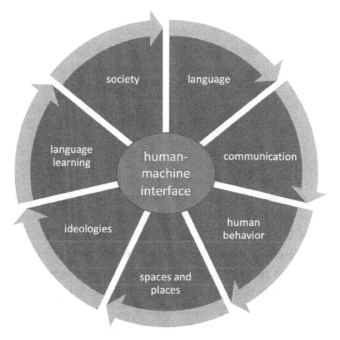

Figure 5 Human-machine research categories

1. **Language**: Machines mediate language in systematic ways, which represents a key area of research to which applied linguistic can offer their expertise. For example, communicating with chatbots may shape how language is used in terms of lexical choice and syntactic complexity. Machines also create new language possibilities, such as the use of emojis and memes alongside text and speech. Furthermore, machines have the ability to influence how humans think about and use languages. For instance, automated translation tools may encourage the use of some languages, such as English, while marginalizing others, such as local competing languages.

2. **Communication**: The human-machine interface presents new ways of communicating, as discussed previously. Designing machines that communicate better with humans, facilitate more efficient communication between humans, and are capable of holding conversations with other machines, requires investigating how such encounters are discursively organized. In other words, applied linguistic scholarship can play a key role in how communication technologies are designed, tested, and implemented, though such contributions require actively seeking interdisciplinary partnerships with researchers working in engineering, HCI, and computer sciences, to name a few.

Caption for Figure 5 (cont.)

3. **Human behavior**: The human-machine interface is transforming patterns of behavior from the mundane and personal to the technical and institutional. The influence machines have on our habit formations comes with an emotional cost. Human interactions with machines can alter our psychological states and well-being, and often in ways that are left unnoticed. Equally important research opportunities are the ways in which machines interact with and shape human behavior, including predicting and tracking our personal and professional actions and practices.

4. **Spaces and places**: The human-machine interface has spatial and geographical consequences. Machines occupy physical spaces, creating meaning in the material world in ways that force humans to alter their behaviors. Self-checkout or check-in kiosks, for example, require humans to interact with machines, which poses numerous empirical questions about new forms of communication. For example, do humans communicate problems or troubles to machines in ways that would be atypical if communicating with a fellow human? Similarly, how are digital spaces creating new ways of thinking and talking about conflict, politics, and culture in both near and far places?

5. **Ideologies**: The human-machine interface continues to transform how humans think about technologies and technological advancements. Online conferencing platforms have, for instance, transformed the ways in which professionals and educators think about occupational spaces and work habits. Similarly, digital platforms that connect contract workers with customers, such as Uber and Airbnb, create unique service encounters that modify how humans think about digital consumerism. In the same vein, the digital economy is radically changing notions of trust, privacy, and reliability.

6. **Language learning**: The human-machine interface is currently altering the ways in which students approach language learning. For instance, the gig economy in general, and online tutoring platforms in particular, provide greater choices for students to select teachers according to language background, geographical location, and language proficiency. VR and AR tools are slowly being introduced into schools, transforming language learning experiences and teaching opportunities. Similarly, machine translation both facilitates and hinders the ability to access and learn languages.

7. **Society**: The human-machine interface presents society with exciting opportunities to exploit technological advancement and innovation. However, such opportunities are attached to social dilemmas, including the ethical implications of using machines to replace humans for core work functions, such as assembly line production, service encounters, transportation, and law.

These seven empirical categories highlight some of the possibilities that exist in researching the human-machine interface. The sample questions and example research topics together demonstrate that applied linguists can contribute much to the study of language and technology. In addition to pursuing new empirical opportunities, applied linguists must approach the human-machine interface with an understanding that is influenced by new ways of thinking about the relationship humans have with technology. In particular, what is needed is a paradigmatic shift in how scholarship views the evolving role machines have in human communication and sociality. This shift is needed given the continued loss in human agency that comes from automation and technological dependency. Posthumanism is one such theoretical framework that can assist in this paradigmatic shift (for a more thorough account of posthumanism, see Wolfe, 2010).

Posthumanism is a philosophical position that rejects an anthropocentric view of human sociality. Posthumanist scholars do not see human sociality as a process for which humans are solely responsible, but is rather part of a larger ecosystem of physical, material, digital, and technological connections.

Posthumanism offers a way of accounting for the changes that come with 4IR technologies. For instance, the realities of gene manipulation, cell printing, and chip implants are upon us, offering concrete and tangible examples of how humans are attached to technology both metaphorically and literally. These realities can be understood by evaluating how humans make sense of the very technologies that mediate their lives. For instance, applied linguistic scholarship can investigate how transformative technologies are discussed by lawmakers and reported on in mainstream media, establishing a better understanding of how societies address the challenges and opportunities that come with revolutionary practices. Neurotechnology is one prime example: this category of technology includes a range of practices from using pharmaceutical drugs to alter the way the mind works to adopting more invasive approaches that include implanting computer systems to communicate directly to the brain. Perhaps the most widely discussed example of neurotechnology in mainstream media is Neuralink, which is a company founded by Elon Musk to capture the true potential of the brain-machine connection. Neuralink is concerned with constructing implantable brain-machine devices to help individuals suffering from paralysis.

Even with less physical and invasive examples of the human-machine interface, such as the ways in which our behaviors are mediated if not controlled by mobile applications and AI tools, posthumanism allows us to see our evolving place in the world through a new lens. For example, posthumanism is framed to investigate how consciousness is increasingly mediated by technological advancements, such as automation, and what these changes mean in a world increasingly dependent on machines. This line of research is critically important in a culture where tasks that were once manned by humans are being replaced by machines.

To this end, scholars working within new materialism have long addressed the ways in which objects in the material world transform consciousness, mental constructions, and other forms of human behavior (for more information on new materialism, see Gamble, Hanan, & Nail, 2019). While new materialism is an interdisciplinary approach with different research trajectories following divergent theoretical positions, it possesses at its core a few defining principles that applied linguists ought to consider in future research on language and technology.

New materialism is an ontological position that views both organic and nonorganic matter as active forces in meaning construction, such as the ways in which humans make sense of the world around them. That is to say, new materialism does not adopt an anthropocentric view of human sociality, but rather sees humans as nonexceptional agents in how the world is organized and understood.

A scholar working within new materialism may study the human-machine interface by uncovering how technology is an active participant in meaning construction. For example, machines are not only part of the material world, but they also mediate how humans occupy physical and digital spaces. Wearable devices, such as a smart watch or a Fitbit, that remind humans to go outside and walk more or to stay inside because of poor weather are two such examples.

The use wearable devices, and in particular the physical and metaphorical link humans and machines share, is a concrete example of why scholarship must seek news ways of understanding language and communication. Entanglement is one such theory that can shed light on the tethered state of humans and machines.

Entanglement is a phenomenon observed in quantum physics in which particles become intertwined and stay linked together even if they travel in opposite directions and remain far away from each other.

Viewing language and communication through the lens of entanglement reveals the complex state of matter and meaning, including the evolution of humans and technology, existing not as "an individual affair" but rather as co-dependent "through and as part of their entangled intra-relating" (Barad, 2007, p. ix).

Seeing humans as one element in a larger constellation of material and digital forces has tremendous implications for the Humanities and its role in the Sciences. Specifically, viewing human sociality through the lens of entanglement forces us to take seriously the contributions the Humanities can make to ongoing technological developments, such as understanding the ethics of automation, the discourse of privacy laws, or the communicative practices of humans working alongside collaborative robots (**cobots**). The significance of such contributions will become more evident as human bodies merge with metal and hardware and algorithms and AI software guide if not program how we think, behave, and communicate.

3 Digital Economies: From Gig Work to Cryptocurrencies

4IR transformations have radically altered the economic landscape in recent years. Such changes have occurred in rapid succession, leaving many individuals and societies unaware of the deep impact technology has made, and will continue to make, in and for the economy. Indeed, basic terminological constructs used to describe and understand the marriage between technology and finance, such as digital economy, are not widely known and seldom used within mainstream society. This lack of understanding is an unfortunate situation to be in for societies, as there are momentous changes occurring within, and significant consequences as a result of, technology and finance. Therefore, establishing a basic understanding of the current state of technology and finance requires defining some basic concepts. To this end, what are digital economies?

Digital economy is a system of economic activities that is conducted online using mobile devices or computers. Digital economies include app-based stock trading, streaming services, e-commerce sites, and cloud computing, to name a few.

The impact technological transformations have on the economy can be thought of in terms of depth and breadth. The rapid and widespread adoption of technological innovation is unprecedented, creating emerging markets and new consumer habits on a global scale. A comparable sweeping transformation occurred in the mid 1990s when the Internet was transformed from a research project studied by few to an open network used by many. The internet boom at the time was transformational in terms of how societies view information and communication, though its economic consequences were far less impactful than what individuals are experiencing in today's economies. For instance, social media is now embedded within, and central to, stock trading, currency investing, mortgage planning, and other banking and financial practices, allowing individuals and institutions to exploit mass communication for monetary gain.

Individuals can make important economic decisions on a phone with a push of a button, and without needing to speak to a human, carving out a financial path according to information shared on social media platforms. Financial institutions have recognized these new consumer habits, creating their own mobile applications that allow users to communicate with each other. This marriage between technology and social media on the one hand, and finance on the other, represents a revolutionary jump from earlier iterations of the Internet, and is often referred to as fintech.

Fintech is a portmanteau of the words finance and technology. The term is used to label or categorize the practice of exploiting technology for financial gain. Fintech applications often make use of AI tools and social media features, allowing individuals and institutions to conduct business with each other and without the need of traditional brick-and-mortar structures.

One of the more concrete examples of the exploitation of technology for financial gain can be found in the transition from permanent full-time workers to fixed and flexible independent contractors. This transition is referred to as the gig economy.

Gig economy is a system of economic activities based on short, paid work performed by independent contractors or freelancers. Gig is colloquial for a one-off "booking" for work, such as a concert gig or a singing gig. Gig work in the digital economy is procured through online platforms or mobile apps, such as Uber.

The gig economy is a hallmark of digital economies, accelerating business opportunities by connecting consumers with potential service providers in ways that are similar to locating friends on social media. Like many aspects of digital economies, however, the gig economy presents societies with a number of moral conundrums. For instance, the gig economy provides consumers with greater purchasing flexibility, as well as access to service providers. Conversely, gig workers have little say in their working conditions and can be easily exploited by poorly defined labor laws that are based on traditional occupational spaces. Such tensions will become more evident as societies continue to invest in a digital economic future (Graham, 2019).

Digital economies must also be thought of in relation to the evolution of web-based business practices. Much has already been said about the Web 2.0 transformations that took place over two decades ago: Online data became increasingly user-generated and participatory over the years. Web 2.0 transformations are still visible in today's economy, including most concretely in the ways in which social media is embedded within business platforms. Despite the presence of Web 2.0 in today's digital economies, the production and management of online data are experiencing radical changes as a result of technological innovation. Such transformations suggest that societies are moving into a new era of the Internet: Web 3.0.

Web 3.0 is the third generation of the Internet. A defining characteristic of Web 3.0 is decentralization. Online data, such as the money exchanged for goods and services, will become increasingly decentralized. Within the context of digital economies, decentralization is simply a process through which business practices move away from a single or central institution or authority, such as central banks. Therefore, third generation digital economies will increasingly rely on decentralized forms of payments, such as cryptocurrencies, as well as infrastructures that support decentralization processes, such as blockchain technology.

Blockchain is a ledger system made up of "blocks" of online data. These blocks contain information about transactions; each block contains a unique identifier, which is stored publicly (rather than centrally). Information stored in blocks are secured through cryptography (e.g., encryption) – for a more detailed and technical description of blockchain technology, see (Pilkington, 2016.). Blockchain technology is the foundation for cryptocurrencies.

Cryptocurrency is a digital system of money. Cryptocurrencies are secured through cryptography, and are thus thought to be a safer and more private form of payment than traditional money circulated through centralized banking institutions – for a more comprehensive discussion of cryptocurrencies, see (Narayanan et al., 2016).

While blockchain technology and cryptocurrencies will continue to grow in societal reach and impact, forcing applied linguists to attend to the ways in which such phenomena mediate language and communication, there are many other digital economic issues that can be addressed in future research. Indeed, it is not difficult to identify what can be investigated in future research from an applied linguistic perspective, as the influence technological transformations have on economies can be found in many domains of life and communicative situations. For instance, digital economies present societies with a number of financial opportunities and challenges from the democratization of cryptocurrencies and the privacy issues that come with tailored services to the exploitation of temporary workers and the loss of jobs through automation.

More concrete examples of research opportunities can be located in how individuals and institutions use technology to make specific business decisions. Technology, for instance, is capable of transforming core business practices, such as hiring and terminating employees, from a deeply human encounter to a profoundly dehumanizing transaction. The actions of Better.com CEO offer an alarming illustration of this type of transformation. At the end of 2021, in the face of increasing financial pressure, the CEO of Better.com held a three-minute Zoom meeting to discuss the current state of the online mortgage company with approximately 15 percent of his employees. Unbeknownst to them, all 900 employees attending the Zoom meeting were to be laid off at the same time, which was done with the following declarative: "If you're on this call, you are part of the unlucky group, that is being laid off, your employment here is terminated effective immediately" (Lock, 2021). This encounter, which was widely circulated on social media after employees shared the recording of the meeting, is not the most cutting-edge example of technology in business; however, the encounter showcases how technology within digital economies can potentially erode human agency by dematerializing occupational spaces.

The impact dematerialization has on humans – daunting as it may seem – is merely a small part of what must be considered when reflecting on, and ultimately researching, digital economies. A more holistic discussion of fintech requires attending to the different aspects of digital economies that are directly relevant to applied linguistic scholarship. These aspects can be summarized as the four Cs of digital economies, as illustrated in Figure 6: constant, communication, customization, and coverage.

The four Cs point to a number of exciting research opportunities to understand the language and communication of digital economies. These opportunities can be divided into two, interrelated categories of investigation: participants and components. Who are the participants of digital economies and how do they make sense of, and participate in, such spaces? Additionally, what components make up digital economies and how do they influence the participants that rely on them? These categories and questions are expressed in Figure 7.

Many of the potentially interesting empirical issues that applied linguists can investigate are related to participants, components, or both categories of investigation. Beyond these empirical possibilities, there are several concerns that applied linguists should attend to when reflecting on, and investigating, digital economies. These concerns, which are illustrated in Figure 8, can be divided into three overlapping areas of concern: privacy, trust, and sustainability.

The key concerns associated with digital economies will be familiar to many business professionals and economists, as privacy, trust, and sustainability have been increasingly topics of discussion within and outside of academic for the last two decades (Shilton & Greene, 2019). This work is important, as it constructs an empirical base to which future scholarship on digital economies can add, including applied linguistic research (e.g., Feng & Ren, 2020). However, the people and components of economies in general, and digital economies in particular, have received far less attention in the applied linguistic literature than topics related to privacy, trust, and sustainability.

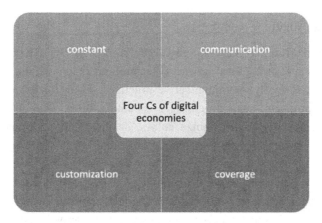

Figure 6 The four Cs of digital economies

1. **Constant**: Digital economies are constantly on, allowing institutions and individuals to engage in business without the need to follow traditional consumer rules and norms, such as closing stores on public holidays or sourcing local products or even services. Always on, however, also means that companies are capable of collecting, and need to collect, data on consumer habits around the clock. Automated tools sit in the background of web browsers, mobile devices, and applications, creating a perpetual state of digital surveillance (Barnard-Wills, 2012). Companies can thus track what individuals purchase and even predict what consumers wish to buy.

2. **Communication**: Digital economies increase communication between and amongst companies and consumers because of social media, AI tools, digitalization processes, and dematerialization outcomes. Many companies now possess a "digital footprint" across many social media platforms, creating a direct channel of communication between institutions and individuals. Autonomous and functional chatbots, which are the outcome of AI tools and the dematerialization of the customer service workforce, make it possible for institutions and individuals to communicate more frequently because robots do not care about business opening hours, time zones, and other human and material concerns. Of course, a central aspect of communicating within digital economies is the sharing of opinions and experiences between consumers on, for example, review websites and other social media platforms (for a study that discusses the connection between political consumerism and social media, see de Zúñiga, Copeland, and Bimber, 2013).

Caption for Figure 6 (cont.)

3. **Customization**: Digital economies lead to increase customization using digital platforms, global partners, technological innovation, AI tools, and transformative communicative practices. Take, for example, consumer products, such as clothing or automobiles. Digital platforms allow consumers to customize colors, designs, and performance features according to their preferences and lifestyles. In general, customizing is easier now than ever before, as businesses can source goods, materials, and services with little regard to region and distance – this observation applies to services as well, such as medicine and language learning where consumers can connect to service providers according to highly individualized preferences (for a study on how language learners can tailor their learning by using tutoring platforms, see Curran, 2020). Technological innovation in automated manufacturing and storage management accelerate the time that it takes to tailor such goods, materials, and services. Furthermore, AI tools predict not only consumer preferences, making recommendations on e-commerce sites for example; but also possible fluctuations in the market, such as a rise or fall in global supply and demand.

4. **Coverage**: Digital economies increase market access and reach. This coverage exists because of the ease in which it is possible to buy and sell goods and services online, reflecting a larger culture of digital consumerism and technological dependency. The culture of digital consumerism exists, in part, because companies recognize that individuals are increasingly spending more time on their mobile devices while engaging in progressively complex and significant financial activities. One historically important technological driving force in digital economies is digital payment systems, which have over the years evolved into an automated tool that is embedded within "non-financial" applications, such as social media and communication platforms. The proliferation of fintech has led to a democratization of financial opportunities, reaching communities that would within traditional financial systems avoid such activities, such as micro-investing (Wang, 2021) in stocks on mobile applications (e.g., Robinhood and Plus500). Furthermore, blockchain technology and cryptocurrencies shift the exchange of money away from large institutions and governments in positions of power; the end result may be a completely decentralized monetary system, though only time will tell if this type of coverage will happen (Mulligan, 2018).

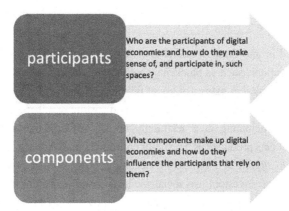

Figure 7 Digital economies research categories

1. **Participants**: The participants of digital economies include consumers, workers, companies, organizations, and industries. Each participant category possesses numerous empirical possibilities from the discursive power that determines participation in digital economies to the language of participants doing finance on e-commerce websites. Take, for example, workers. Digital economies present applied linguists with many real-world problems that deserve further empirical scrutiny, such as the ways in which workers use language to express professional ambitions in the face of increasing specialization, reflect on the extent to which they possess autonomy and agency at their workplace, and confront the working standards that define the parameters from which they can earn money and make a living. In some professions, such as language teaching, these real-world problems have been shown to play an important role in how digital workers complete basic occupational duties. For example, online tutoring platforms that connect language learners with prospective teachers allow students to select instructors according to a number of categories, including language background, nationality, and education, to name a few. While this variety gives students greater autonomy in their learning, it can encourage teachers to reinforce problematic neoliberal discourses and construct native speakerism ideologies that are harmful to the profession (Curran, 2021).

2. **Components**: The components of digital economies are the instruments and modes of exchange. The instruments of exchange are the currencies, commodities, and securities that are used to purchase and sell goods and services. Digital economies are mediated by these instruments, such as cryptocurrencies (e.g., Dogecoin) and NTFs (i.e., nonfungible tokens). In this sense, digital economies are no different than traditional economies. Both economies rely on financial instruments that possess monetary value. However, digital economies make use of different modes of exchange, such as social media. These modes of exchange

Caption for Figure 7 (cont.)

are managed in and through online channels that are propped up by techno-logical innovations, such as blockchain technology. Instruments and modes of exchange are central to many aspects of life that concern applied linguists from the power structures between individuals and institutions that get altered as a result of participating in a seemingly borderless economic space to the language that gets produced as a result of consumers making sense of emerging trends within digital economies. For example, how does a community of ostensibly casual investors use social media to communicate a plan to resist and confront the profit-making strategies of powerful financial institutions responsible for trading securities? The answer to this question lies in a recent example of Reddit users banding together to purchase or hold Gamestop stocks, knowing that this strategy would go against, and ultimately lose money for, powerful and established financial institutions (Chohan, 2021).

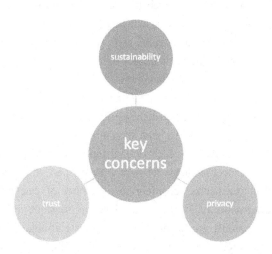

Figure 8 Primary concerns associated with digital economies

1. **Privacy** is a topic of discussion for many stakeholders in digital economies. This is because digital economies are dependent on the collection, aggregation, and application of consumer data. For example, the ability to tailor goods and services according to individual preferences is based on consumer data. Big data technologies, such as data mining algorithms, are capable of running in the background of webpages while consumers browse the Internet, collecting and transforming data for financial gain. While many consumers have grown accustomed to individualized and automated services, there are increasingly

Caption for Figure 8 (cont.)

significant privacy risks that come with the technologies of growing digital economies. Identity theft and loss, as well as the misuse of consumer data, are significant concerns for societies that applied linguists can investigate.

2. **Trust** is a major concern within digital economies; in particular, trust is declining in digital economies, as businesses are increasingly dependent on the collection and application of consumer data for financial gain. A general skepticism within societies regarding the morality of profit-making companies has already existed for some time now (see, for example, Hemphill, 2002)). More recently, trust continues to erode because of the many criticisms that have been directed at the neoliberal structures in which powerful institutions, such banks and trading companies, are embedded (Baldwin, 2018). Consequences of participating in digital economies, such as extensive security beaches, add to the decline of trust. With that said, however, other aspects of digital economies can promote trust. For example, social media platforms are embedded within, as well as host, many businesses, allowing consumers to share and disseminate information about unscrupulous individuals and businesses or unethical and perhaps even illegal business practices. Gig economy platforms, such as Airbnb, are designed according to an information-sharing ethos, permitting an ostensibly open dialogue between consumers and service providers that is meant to encourage transparency and trust. Despite this objective, gig economy scholars argue that the algorithms used on such platforms can in practice silence and prevent customers and service providers from doing business in equitable and sustainable ways (Kellogg, Valentine, & Christin, 2020).

3. **Sustainability** is central to how digital economies grow alongside 4IR transformations. Similarly, digital economies are central to how, and to what extent, societies can and wish to engage in sustainable efforts. The relationship between economic viability and development on the one hand, and sustainability on the other hand, is most pronounced in efforts to protect, or in some cases, ignore, the environment. Economies anchored to digital technologies are no different. While the common assumption is that digital transformations can lead to greater sustainable efforts by moving away from traditional emission-based resources (e.g., increasing efficiency in manufacturing as a result of technological innovation), the truth is that 4IR transformations are entangled in many sustainability challenges both old and new. For instance, technological innovations can lead to better tools for tracking sustainability progress and environmental impact. However, such tools, such as the hardware components required to run complex tracking calculations, are tied to vulnerable and often scarce human, economic, and environmental resources.

More specifically, matters related to the economy have received some attention in applied linguistic research (Ricento, 2015), though much of the work done is related to neoliberalism (e.g., Block, Gray, & Holborow, 2012). For example, a search on Linguistics and Language Behavior Abstracts using the keywords "neoliberalism" or "political economy" yielded over 200 peer-reviewed publications from 1974 to 2022. Although 200 publications over five decades of scholarship amount to a small body of research, the number is much larger than the amount of published work on digital economies. Searching the same database with the keywords "digital economy" or "digital economies" resulted in only six peer-reviewed publications from 1999 to 2020.

Both search results are intriguing given how closely connected the economy is to sustainability efforts. Furthermore, both search results demonstrate that there are numerous digital economic issues that applied linguists can investigate. Such issues intersect with most of the topics presented in this Element thus far, and can be studied according to any of the categories of research identified previously. For example, returning to Figure 2, digital economies can be studied as one of the following social processes: mediation, systems, and order. For mediation, applied linguists can study how issues of trust in AI tools is discursively expressed in online service encounters. Similarly, order can be investigated by looking at the language used to establish the legal and economic boundaries of what is acceptable levels of privacy, trust, and sustainability. Also of concern for applied linguists is systems, and the ways in which technological innovation, such as wearable devices that monitor heart data, may influence how participants of digital economies make sense of health service professionals.

This section has established the importance of digital economies, and their relevance to applied linguistic research (for an in-depth discussion of the value in investigating social class, see Block, 2013). Digital economies will continue to grow in reach and impact, creating an even larger empirical lacuna than what presently exists within the applied linguistic literature. Greater attention to technological innovation in digital economies will help address many of the opportunities and threats that exist within and across today's increasingly interconnected societies.

4 Communicating Threats: Security Breaches, Language Injustices, Civil Subjugation, and Other Dangers

4IR transformations bring exciting opportunities to advance societies in sustainable and democratic ways, as demonstrated in previous sections. Some of the many advancements include the ways in which biofabrication will transform the potential of the human body, using 3D cell printing and biocompatible materials to create functional living tissues. Similarly, advances in brain-machine implants will allow paralysis sufferers to enjoy a better life, radically altering what is it means to live with technology. New ways of experiencing human sociality are being introduced through VR and AR tools, merging physical and digital spaces to allow geographically displaced friends and family to interact as if they were physically co-present. Hardware devices connected to the Internet bring new possibilities in managing, and having more control over, mundane life tasks, such as monitoring vital house statistics or adjusting cooking appliances on a mobile device.

These examples demonstrate that efforts to accelerate technological innovation can be tied to positive outcomes. Take, for example, ongoing efforts to offer internet access to developing countries, which is central to 4IR advancements. A recent report contends that 4.3 billion people do not have internet access, which amounts to nearly 60 percent of the world population (West, 2015). This is a staggering number given the economic, social, and educational opportunities and benefits that are afforded to individuals with internet access. Furthermore, access to economic, social, and educational possibilities will be increasingly mediated through the Internet and other online, app-based platforms as societies continue to depend on technology (European Commission, 2022). According to the Agency of Healthcare Research and Quality (2021), internet access contributes to well-being in numerous ways, including most notably in healthcare systems that are committed to digitalization. It is therefore sensible, if not morally obligatory, to devote much energy and resources into providing internet access to all that wish to have it.

Yet, mass production and technological innovation, two important factors in providing affordable and reliable internet access to rural communities and developing countries, are entangled in the exploitation of human labor, depletion of natural resources, commercialization of public services, violation of financial laws, and marginalization of cultural and linguistic groups (for a study of the potential links between economic growth and the environment, see Andrée et al., 2019). While internet access is only one of many issues that must be addressed as societies move deeper into digital spaces, these entangled threats are part and parcel of 4IR life.

The point in presenting this bleak characterization is that 4IR celebrations – which this Element can be considered – must be tempered with an acknowledgement of the antagonistic forces that come with the benefits of technological transformations. In other words, a section that focuses on these associative threats is needed to provide a balanced overview of 4IR.

To this end, the current section offers a glimpse into some of the threats that come with 4IR change and innovation.

Numerous threats are entangled in 4IR change and innovation, including most notably for applied linguists the social and linguistic issues that are tied to technology, such as language change and cultural inequality. Translation tools, for instance, transform notions of reading literacy, but do so while privileging the languages of powerful nations in general, and English in particular (for an older, but relevant discussion, see Cronin, 1998). Additionally, the collection, management, and commodification of user data are issues that intersect with a plethora of empirical topics that concern applied linguists. For example, user data are central to how individuals discursively construct notions of privacy, as Georgalou's (2016) study on Facebook users demonstrates. Furthermore, understanding how 4IR transformations impact human life requires a high level of technical literacy that is difficult to teach in schools (Iivari et al., 2016). This literacy gap will widen if 4IR technologies continue to advance with little to no educational support directed at teaching younger generations about 4IR transformations.

Beyond these stated threats, there are a number of existential challenges for societies. Establishing a research agenda based on 4IR threats is nonetheless difficult, as they are both pervasive and nebulous. For example, criticisms of globalist policies, including those related to the World Economic Forum and Klaus Schwab (e.g., the Great Reset), are rooted in a long history of justifiable distrust of power institutions that disperse into fragmented beliefs systems that find their way onto social media platforms and may even evolve into conspiratorial discourse. Furthermore, while threats are discussed in both mainstream media and scholarship, they are not often framed as 4IR entanglements. Contextualizing threats within broader historical and evolutionary discussions is needed to understand 4IR challenges as interconnected and consequential phenomena. Some of the many threats that are relevant to applied linguists, but are not often framed as 4IR issues, include climate change, job insecurity, cybersecurity, privacy, language representation, censorship, troll farms, cancel culture, fake news, and conspiracy theories.

Rather than list all empirical issues that are mediated by 4IR innovation and change, which does not offer a practical way of establishing a research agenda, this section identifies five interrelated categories that encapsulate 4IR threats: rights, information, control, representation, and security. Collectively, these five categories offer a compelling account of what must be done socially, linguistically, and empirically. Figure 9 provides an illustration of these five threats for easy reference.

While these five interrelated threats present an ominous account of technological innovation and change, each threat should be viewed as an opportunity

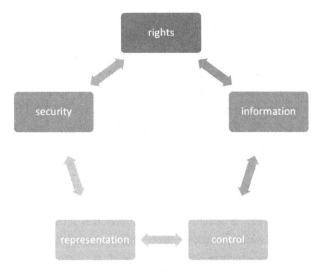

Figure 9 Five threats

1. **Rights** are human entitlements that all individuals are afforded in society regardless of their economic and cultural profiles. Basic human rights include, but are not limited to, the right to education, the right to live, and the right to express an opinion. Some aspects of technology threaten human rights, such as the complicated relation between automation and the right to work. For instance, although automation increases productivity and efficiency, research suggests that individuals have mixed feelings about the widespread use of AI (Araujo et al., 2020). Other threats to human rights that stem from 4IR innovation and change include intellectual property rights, defamation, censorship, and human exploitation, to name a few (for a fuller discussion of AI and human rights, see Risse, 2018). While numerous threats to human rights exist, of particular concern and relevance to 4IR technologies are digital footprints, which are defined as the information based on an individual's online activity. The ability to take control, or possess some ownership over, digital footprints is being taken away by corporations and institution that seek to use the information to engage in different business practices, such as using personal data for contact tracing purposes in the context of the COVID-19 pandemic (Guinchard, 2021). The right to access, control, and take ownership over, such information is a key area of future applied linguistic research, as digital footprints intersect with other 4IR threats.

2. **Information** in the age of 4IR transformations is a major threat to societies, as technology is the primary medium through which knowledge is created and shared. While technology is not inherently partial to social and cultural ideas and beliefs, humans can be biased, are sometimes criminal, and have been historically incredibly prejudiced. The use of technology to create, disseminate, and consume information in the age of 4IR transformations has the potential to

Caption for Figure 9 (cont.)

facilitate some of these biases, criminal inclinations, and prejudiced behaviors. Technology can, for example, collect private and sensitive information from unknowing individuals and institutions, facilitate the rapid dissemination of unfiltered knowledge (and misinformation) with great reach, and be presented as an objective medium through which important decisions are made, such as with credit reports, student grades, and legal behavior. Information that is of particular concern within the context of 4IR transformations fall under one of two categories: misinformation and no information. Misinformation is related to fake news (e.g., fictitious reports of war or crime) and mock news (e.g., entertainment presented as news). No information is related to transparency, and the extent to which personal data are shared or made available to the very individuals to which such information is related. Technology can facilitate the use of misinformation and the practice of no information.

3. **Control** is the threat of subjugation, which is an issue of increasing concern given the amount of information that exists in digital spaces and the extent to which societies rely on such data. Of particular concern is the sharp increase in the use of **ransomware**, which is an application that steals or conceals information for the purpose of demanding a ransom. While institutions and companies are typically the target of larger ransom demands, individuals are often victims of cyber extortion. Technological advancements will create more sophisticated attacks in the future, which leads to further subjugation in that societies are forced to alter the way information is managed online as a result of such threats. Applied linguists can contribute to the study of control and cyber-attacks by looking at the rhetorical strategies used by the media when reporting on such crimes or the discursive construction of demands by criminal organizations. Most reports suggest that cyber-attacks pose a serious threat to societies committed to the digitalization of information, as there have been sharp increases in most forms of online criminal behavior in recent years (see, for example, Federal Bureau of Investigation, 2020). The threat of control is not limited to people subjugating people: Subjugation can also happen when people alter their behavior because of machines. Familiar examples of machines subjugating people include, but are not limited to, the ways in which wearable technology (e.g., health monitors), notifications (e.g., reminders), and gamification features (e.g., language learning apps) compel humans to alter their behavior as a result of information gathered through such devices and applications.

4. **Representation** refers to the ways in which cultures are presented and used in online spaces. Cultural and linguistic representations are a threat to societies for some of the reasons identified in previous threats, such as the ability to transmit

unfiltered information (e.g., racialized discourses) to a large audience with little to no consequence. A key concern is how stereotypes of cultures can be reinforced in and though technology. For instance, it is not uncommon for cultural groups to be misrepresented on social media: This is often done by creating fictitious events associated with, or ascribing undesirable qualities to, marginalized communities. The portrayal of migrants as dangerous or a threat to the core values of a country is one such example (A. Bhatia & Jenks, 2018). 4IR advancements, such as **synthetic media** (commonly known as "deep fakes"), make it easier to create misrepresentations, which disrupt harmony and cohesion within and across societies. Digital reliance and online communication make it difficult to distinguish between genuine and fictitious information in other more mundane ways, as it is easy to create fake user accounts, portray oneself as a legitimate authority figure, and characterize or represent cultural groups in problematic and erroneous ways. Although misrepresentation is a major threat to societies, it is also important to attend to the issue of underrepresentation. For example, Big Tech companies like Apple and Google have neglected (and continue to neglect) African (and other widely used) languages in automated translation and speech recognition technologies, privileging instead the Americas, Europe, and Asia, including the lesser used languages of such regions, such as Icelandic (see, for example, Young, 2015).

5. **Security** in the age of 4IR transformations is a threat to all levels of societies and in multiple domains of life from large multinational corporations and government websites to the bank accounts of ordinary individuals and social media passwords. Numerous factors have accelerated the need to secure personal or sensitive data, including in recent years concerted efforts by companies to tailor online experiences for customers and companies encouraging flexible remote working opportunities during the global pandemic. Both examples lead to an increase in online activity, creating larger digital footprints and greater possibilities for security breaches. As with all threats discussed in this section, technological advancements allow criminals to carry out increasingly sophisticated security breaches, such as monitoring home monitoring devices to determine when homeowners are away. The amount of money spent on protecting sensitive data, and the financial losses as a result of security breaches, are staggering. In US manufacturing alone, for example, industry losses in 2016 were at least $8 billion and potentially up to $36 billion (Thomas, 2020). Security threats also come from tracking and surveillance applications, which are partly designed to prevent criminal activity. However, such applications can give a false sense of security, increase skepticism in institutions, and ultimately provide more opportunities for data theft.

to shape future language and communication research. Yet, applied linguists must collectively determine the composition of a research agenda on the language and communication of 4IR threats. That is to say, it is beyond the scope of this Element to identify the precise empirical topics that should be published in journals and as books. It is, on the other hand, feasible and necessary to discuss 4IR threats in a way that is more palatable to applied linguists. To this end, one way of making sense of 4IR threats from a language and communication perspective is to think about who communicates such dangers. That is, who is communicating 4IR threats and how is this being accomplished? Three possibilities exist: individuals, industries, and institutions. Figure 10 offers an illustration of communicating 4IR threats.

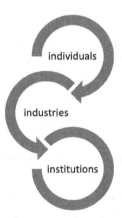

Figure 10 Communicating threats

1. **Individuals** are ordinary members of society that express their concerns for different societal threats, including 4IR dangers. This form of communicating threats is most impactful when individuals use digital tools and online spaces to express a particular concern, influencing readers beyond the physical boundaries of ordinary face-to-face communication. In this sense, technology gives individuals a degree of power that did not exist two decades ago when efforts to communicate threats were limited to small social groups and family members. An important empirical topic relates to how individuals exploit technological tools to communicate 4IR threats. For example, how does technology mediate the ways in which individuals express concerns over technological innovation and change? Varis (2019), for instance, explores how online memes are used to articulate mostly North American inspired conspiracy theories. Future research

Caption for Figure 10 (cont.)

can build on this revelatory study by examining how more advanced technologies, such as synthetic media, are used to construct and share conspiracy theories from and beyond the North American context.

2. **Industries** are businesses, mainstream media, finance, health services, education, and other industrial groups that are entangled in, and committed to, 4IR transformations. Although all industrial groups, along with their affiliated companies, communicate 4IR threats in myriad ways, information technology is the most obvious topic of investigation for applied linguists. Information technology is an industrial group, which includes some of the more commonly known Big Tech companies like Microsoft, Apple and Google, that is responsible for, and the source of, what and how 4IR threats are circulated and communicated within and across societies. Big Tech companies in particular must receive greater empirical scrutiny, as they are almost never a topic of investigation in applied linguistic journals and only tangentially attended to in discussions of technology. Some of the many examples of 4IR threats related to Big Tech companies include user data management services, antitrust (or market competition) laws, censorship practices, national security threats, human exploitation in business practices, and monopolistic tendencies. Such topics can be investigated by looking at how Big Tech companies discursively navigate such threats within the context of product-and-service promotion.

   Alternatively, it is important to look at how industries in general, and Big Tech companies in particular, position themselves in relation to 4IR threats.

3. **Institutions** are cultural spaces that are historically rooted in, and responsible for future changes made to, the development and management of societies, such as the family and the state. As with individuals and industries, institutions are entangled in 4IR transformations: Institutions participate in technological innovation and change, but are also shaped by the very technologies for which they are responsible. For example, governments are incentivized to promote technological innovation and change, as 4IR transformations lead to economic growth and create new job opportunities. In so doing, governments are perpetually responding to the societal consequences that come with new forms of technology, such as creating new laws that protect individuals from online criminal behavior. In this sense, institutions are partly responsible for the very 4IR threats for which they express concerns. Of particular interest within the domain of institutions and technology is the discourse of digital laws. Analyzing the laws of 4IR technologies (e.g., privacy laws, copyright laws, criminal laws, banking laws) is an area of research that applied linguists can make a significant contribution, as the field has a rich tradition of analyzing such language in different

Caption for Figure 10 (cont.)

contexts (e.g., V. Bhatia, Candlin, & Engberg, 2008). How institutions communicate the threats related to 4IR transformations is a fruitful area of research for another important reason: The study of institutions, including the discourse analysis of law, is interdisciplinary in nature, providing a logical and natural path to collaboration with researchers working in other fields of study (for an interdisciplinary take on the language of fear, see Cap, 2017). Interdisciplinary work that builds on the work done in, for example, computer science, engineering, health communication, or law is one of several opportunities that applied linguists can explore to make substantive contributions to the study of 4IR transformations (for a more detailed discussion of what applied linguists can do in future research, see Section 6).

Investigating how the threats associated with technology are communicated is foundational to building a comprehensive understanding of 4IR transformations, yet the study of such communicative practices also contributes to the literature on language and society in more general ways. That is, in communicating 4IR threats, individuals, industries, and institutions reveal a great deal about the culture of societies, including the social dilemmas of a country, the challenges facing a particular community, and the concerns of ordinary people. Indeed, communicating 4IR threats is an empirical topic that concerns public discourses, perceptions, and values. The issue of power, which includes anyone and anything from organizations in positions of power to individuals with little to no voice in society, predictably shapes the ways in which public discourses are constructed and circulated within and across communities (for a seminal publication on power and discourse, see van Dijk, 1993), which is a topic of discussion presented in the next section.

5 Systems of Power: Regulating Information and Communication

A system of power is defined as an influence or control over a person, thing, or issue. In this sense, a system of power is no different than the singular use of power, though the latter, more prototypical term is not used in this section because it does not adequately capture the interconnected nature of power within societies, especially within the context of 4IR transformations. Systems of power come from systemic inequalities (e.g., access to health and education), social hierarchies (e.g., wealth and class), and cultural dynamics (e.g., race relations and political disagreements).

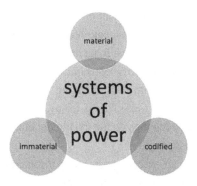

Figure 11 Systems of power

Different domains of life are shaped by systems of power. For example, income inequality creates a system of power that plays out in society in a number of ways, including access to goods and services, language and communicative practices, educational attainment, and health and well-being. Systems of power may be material (e.g., access to private doctors and hospitals, human trafficking, government assistance, prison systems, military force), immaterial (e.g., unspoken stereotypes, belief systems, values, spoken language), or codified (e.g., immigration laws, mission statements, community rules, graffiti art). These modes of power, which are visually depicted in Figure 11, are a reminder that systemic inequalities, social hierarchies, and cultural dynamics can be found at all levels of society and located in every domain of life.

Systems of power entangled in 4IR transformations can be found in material, immaterial, and codified settings and contexts, as will be demonstrated in this section. In the context 4IR transformations, the issue of how information and communication are regulated is important to an understanding of systems of power.

One such example of power relates to technological knowledge, and the ways in which it is used to exert control over people, things, and issues. Technological knowledge is the procedural and declarative competences that are needed to understand and use technology. Continued 4IR transformations require societies to develop technological knowledge (e.g., technical skills, digital literacy, programming language), as the ability to live a meaning life will be increasingly dependent on specialized and technical procedural and declarative competences. System inequalities entangled in 4IR transformations come from a range of setting and contexts, including the growing relationship between humans and machines, internet experiences, online data management, and access to information, to name a few.

Like many aspects of life from education to wealth, technological knowledge exists within a hierarchy: Individuals, communities, and societies have different levels of access to, and competences in, technology. These disparities in access and competences harden and stratify as technology evolves into more complex phenomena and maps out onto long-standing systemic inequalities, social hierarchies, and cultural dynamics. That is to say, systemic inequalities, social hierarchies, and cultural dynamics do not exist independently, but are all part of a network of complex issues.

Although technology can exacerbate systemic inequalities, harden social hierarchies, and problematize cultural dynamics, humans are ultimately responsible for these processes. That is, humans imprint their own systems of power onto technology. Put differently, technology does not possess a desire to exert power over people and humanly things. One way of understanding the power dynamics between humans and technology is to consider the human needs that are tied to 4IR transformations. To this end, systems of power that are entangled in 4IR transformations can be located in three, overlapping human needs: communication, belonging, and information (for a different, but related, account of how the relationship between humans and technology plays out in society, see Haff, 2014). These human needs are graphically depicted in Figure 12.

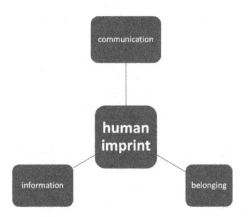

Figure 12 Human imprint

1. **The need to communicate**: This need can establish systems of power onto technology. While technologies enhance communication possibilities, providing, for example, more opportunities to understand and convey meaning, their development and application are founded on established systemic inequalities, social hierarchies, and cultural dynamics. For example, automated translation makes it possible to communicate across many linguistic

Caption for Figure 12 (cont.)

contexts, but such technologies are based on long-standing linguistic prejudices, such as notions of what is an important language.

Additionally, the need to communicate establishes systems of power by relying on communication technologies that police information according to principles that may not be shared by all members of society. In the context of automated translation, such technologies regulate information by determining what languages are available for translation and dictating how translated utterances should be constructed. Similarly, social media platforms regulate information by creating community guidelines regarding what can and cannot be said. This control over how communication must take place creates a system of power that dictates what is socially and pragmatically acceptable ways of communicating.

2. **The need to belong**: The need to belong can establish systems of power onto technology. While technology provides greater opportunities to socialize, form communities, and connect with distant friends and family, the need to belong is also tied to a primordial desire to be loyal and fear others. As a result, communication mediated by technology always has the potential to be tribal, confrontational, inflammatory, and argumentative. The question of whether these features of communication should be ignored, permitted, or rejected is central to systems of power. For example, social media platforms allow users to discuss long-standing societal issues and problems, but algorithms that automate and tailor online experiences reward information that is controversial or confrontational. Therefore, 4IR transformations create opportunities for societies to confront, but also exacerbate, existing social problems. Determining what groups and ideas are acceptable, tolerable, or undesirable creates, but also feeds off of established, systems of power. For example, individuals (e.g., members of political parties), industries (e.g., Big Tech), and institutions (e.g., the Christian family) in positions of power will invariably control, or directly influence, how societies create, disseminate, and make sense of anything from mundane social issues to complex political matters. Thus, forming social groups can be a political endeavor that is influenced by dominant ideologies.

3. **The need for information**: This need can establish systems of power onto technology. While technology provides greater opportunities to create and share information, humans must rely on machines in order to regulate such data. The issue of information regulation is important to the future of human sociality and communication. For example, societies dependent on 4IR innovation and change are entangled in a web of tools and applications

Caption for Figure 12 (cont.)

that track and manage information, as it is impossible for humans to search through, and curate, a growing repository of knowledge, data, and online content. As a result, there is growing demand for AI tools that can search through and manage information so that online experiences are streamlined and individualized. Indeed, online experiences and internet browsing are already structured on information management systems that are programmed to run with little to no human involvement. Individuals, industries, and institutions can exploit this situation by using technologies to exert power within a range of social contexts, including enacting laws that are favorable to profit-making organizations, stealing personal or sensitive information, establishing troll farms, and creating division within and across communities.

While these three needs establish that humans imprint their own subjectivities and biases onto technology, technological innovation and change require societies to place a great deal of trust in machines while giving up human agency. Relying on technologies to complete anything from mundane personal tasks to complex state-level projects means societies will be increasingly in the clutches of technology: Current and concrete examples include, but are certainly not limited to, using machines to determine threats to society, trusting software applications to evaluate sensitive information, and relying on automation for personal and public transportation.

The cost of relying on 4IR transformations is not limited to human agency. Using technology to mediate and facilitate communication can establish alternative realities and false narratives that are inherently divisive. For instance, video-sharing websites and social media platforms, such as YouTube and Twitter, are the primary sources of information, news, and knowledge for many individuals and communities (Rosentiel, 2012). These websites and platforms make use of automation and AI tools to curate information so that online experiences are tailored to individual preferences. The upshot is that if a user subscribes to a particular set of political ideologies, then technology is programmed to curate related information to props up such belief systems. While this situation is no different than how humans form social groups in the physical world, technology accelerates and amplifies these processes by giving voice to fringe theories, a platform for hate speech, and credence to fictitious information while simultaneously making it easy for individuals of such beliefs to meet likeminded people. Consequently, digital spaces for communication can easily transform into echo chambers despite the wealth of competing ideas that are available online.

Echo chamber is a space that reinforces and insulates ideologies by preventing users from needing to address opposing ideas, creating distinct communicative practices and lexical choice.

The societal consequences of echo chambers have been discussed somewhat extensively in communication and media studies (e.g., Flaxman, Goel, & Rao, 2016): not surprisingly, research finds that communication within echo chambers is often negative (Andersson, 2021), and the language used by ·biased groups possesses homophilic elements (Williams et al., 2015).

Homophily is a sociological theory that is often used in networking studies; the theory contends that humans form groups according to the characteristics, attitudes, values, and experiences that they possess or with which they are familiar.

The way information is regulated within and across ideological groups is central to how systems of power entangled in 4IR transformations function. With little to no built-in mechanisms that mediate and regulate information in digital communication spaces (e.g., peer review, fact checks, data filters), ideological groups can easily disseminate fictitious information for political objectives, deepening divides between communities, encouraging uncritical thinking, and creating additional and unnecessary content for debate, fear, and coercion.

Systems of power may also be utilized by ideological groups to organize civic activities, form protests, and even conduct attacks. Although systems of power can be used in positive ways, such as confronting problematic social issues on social media (e.g., addressing racial discrimination and raising awareness about climate change), harmful applications of technology present more urgent issues for societies to address. The Capitol Hill insurrection on January 6, 2021, is one such example. Specifically, the attack on, and riots around, the Capitol building provide a recent reminder of how language and communication are central to systems of power entangled in 4IR transformations.

The misinformation created and circulated on digital platforms leading up to the Capitol Hill attack, especially with regard to election fraud, played a pivotal role in how the events on January 6, 2021, unfolded. On Facebook alone, over 650,000 messages were posted over this period with 10,000 posts per day, all questioning the outcome of the presidential election (Silverman et al., 2022). Fueled with misinformation and inflammatory opinions, extreme factions of Trump supporters used social media to organize armed protests around the United States, including Capitol Hill. Misinformation was further legitimized when individuals in positions of power, including political officials and the then president, refused to accept the official results of the election.

The systems of power that facilitated the discussions leading up to, and the activities of, the Capitol Hill attacks extend beyond January 6, 2021. The decision of Twitter, Facebook, and YouTube to ban President Donald Trump from their platforms is one of the most consequential examples of powerful institutions exerting their influence over society. Questions pertaining to who is capable of censoring, who should be censored, what language is used to justify censorship, and how censorial discourses apply to ordinary members of society will shape the future of digital communication for many years to come.

That is to say, the regulation of information and communication will, and should, become a central public issue for many societies, as language and communicative practices are integral to how systems of power are propped up and enforced.

The issues presented in this section offer a window into how systems of power are entangled in the regulation of information and communication. These issues can also be expressed as questions that future applied linguistic research can address.

Several questions are related to how the regulation of information and communication feed into systems of power, which are presented in the following list.

1. **Who regulates information and communication?** Understanding how the regulation of information and communication feeds into, and is influenced by, systems of power requires identifying and examining the individuals, industries, and institutions responsible for such regulatory practices.

2. **Who is the target of information and communication regulations?** Understanding how the regulation of information and communication feeds into, and is influenced by, systems of power also requires identifying and examining the individuals, industries, and institutions that are the target of such regulatory practices.

3. **How is information and communication regulated?** The ways in information and communications are regulated, such as through state policies or censorship practices, are central to an understanding how systems of power are entangled in 4IR transformations.

4. **What are the social and linguistic implications of regulation?** The power dynamics that are involved in the regulation of information and communication manifest in society in a number of social and linguistic ways. Understanding these manifestations will help shed light on the ways in which systems of power are entangled in 4IR transformations.

In addition to these questions, several concluding observations can be made to summarize systems of power. First, systems of power are entangled in 4IR transformations. Second, technology is inextricably connected to long-standing systemic inequalities, social hierarchies, and cultural dynamics. Thus, locating how systems of power are entangled in 4IR transformations will help confront societal issues that have existed for millennia. Third, and relatedly, technology is not inherently biased; however, humans imprint their own power dynamics onto, and with the use of, technology. Fourth, systems of power entangled in 4IR transformations can be found at all levels of society and located in every domain of life.

6 Conclusion: The Role of Applied Linguistics

The beginning of this Element contended that a necessary first step in tracking the ways in which technology is transforming human language and communication is to establish a terminological base from which future applied linguistic scholarship can exploit. This first step was established in this Element by identifying a number of terms and constructs that applied linguists can apply in future research, including 4IR, phygital, biofabrication, bots, and digital economies. These and other terms and constructs (e.g., Hancock, Naaman, & Levy, 2020) are not merely ornamental or symbolic attempts to acknowledge ongoing technological transformations. Such terms and constructs help frame salient, but more importantly current, language and technology themes while locating allied empirical issues relevant to applied linguistic scholarship.

In addition to identifying terms and constructs, this Element identified numerous research topics that applied linguists should investigate, categorizing and thus formalizing an empirical agenda dedicated to 4IR innovation and change. Some of the more notable topics that were identified in this Element are modes of human-machine communication, the human-machine interface, the four Cs of digital economies, and 4IR threats.

Applied linguists are well-placed to carve out a research agenda within the study of modes of human-machine communication. The bulk of work in this area comes from scholarly traditions with little formal history in the study of language, linguistics, and communication (e.g., Yin et al., 2021). Applied linguists can study, for example, the communication of, and the language used within, human-machine-human, human-machine, machine-human, and machine-machine participatory structures. The study of chatbots in particular, such as ChatGPT, is a particularly exciting opportunity for applied linguists to actively contribute to the literature on language and technology.

The human-machine interface is an area of study that is made up of numerous investigatory themes that are relevant to applied linguistic scholarship, including the behavior of humans in machine contexts and the ways in which language and communication are shaped by such encounters. Applied linguistic scholarship is in a privileged position to understand the spaces and places that mediate human-machine communication, such as human encounters with chat-bots, the use of automated translation tools to communicate with interlocutors that do not share a common language, and the online platforms that bring geographically diverse individuals together to engage in trade and commerce.

Furthermore, the four Cs of digital economies intersect with several language and communication issues that have in recent years received much attention in the applied linguistic literature; these aspects of digital economies include the constant state of digital economies, the communication that shapes notions of what is good for the economy, the customization qualities that are based on automation technologies that allow for even more individualism within com-merce, and the market coverage that is attained through digital platforms.

Of particular concern for human language and communication are 4IR threats, which are entangled in numerous societal challenges, including climate change, job insecurity, cybersecurity, privacy, language representation, censor-ship, troll farms, cancel culture, fake news, and conspiracy theories. These threats can be categorized into a number of different, yet overlapping issues, such as the rights afforded to humans in digital spaces, the information that is collected online and used for commercial purposes, the control that is acquired and relinquished when relying on AI, the representation of cultures in auto-mated language tools, and the security that is built around the platforms that societies rely on for anything from mundane tasks to highly complex institu-tional transactions.

The collection of terms, constructs, and empirical categories identified in this Element comes from the urgent need to uncover the impact 4IR transformations have on human language and communication. This need to understand ongoing technological changes is best formulated and summarized by returning to the three aspects of 4IR transformations discussed by Schwab (2016) in his seminal book on the topic: velocity, breadth and depth; system impact.

1. **Velocity**: Technological advancements are accelerating at an unfathomable rate, leaving a growing void of knowledge to fill. In general, applied linguistic scholarship has not sufficiently investigated how societies are being shaped by cutting-edge technology. Several fields of study that are dedicated to understanding technology and human communication exist, providing opportunities for applied linguists to offer language expertise to scholars already working with cutting-edge technologies, such as HCI (for an HCI study that investigates smart home applications, see Alao, Joshua, & Akinsola, 2019). Keeping pace with technological advancements requires knowing and using the terms and constructs associated with 4IR

technologies. However, being cognizant of, and drawing from, 4IR terms and constructs will not slow down technological advancements, but such knowledge will help applied linguists contribute to future changes and deal with eminent threats.

2. **Breadth and depth**: In addition to pace, technological advancements are reaching more domains of life while making larger and deeper imprints on members of society. Understanding such imprints require more complex and interdisciplinary approaches and frameworks. Although applied linguistic scholarship is inherently interdisciplinary, applied linguists can seek new partnerships with technology scholars in their pursuit to understand empirical issues related, but not limited to, breadth and depth. One such partnership includes *science and technology studies* (STS), which is itself an interdisciplinary field of study dedicated to understanding the intersection between technology and society (see, for example, Sismondo, 2010). Such partnerships will enable applied linguists to better understand breadth and depth by taking on new ways of mapping out the extent to which life is transforming because of technological advancements, which are matters to which STS scholars are dedicated.

3. **Systems impact**: Velocity, breadth, and depth result in a grid of interconnected communities and societies that are increasingly dependent on each other, as well as 4IR technologies. Similar observations are made by scholars using *actor network theory*, which offers a useful theoretical framework for applied linguists seeking answers to questions pertaining to how technology creates social and digital connections within and across communities and societies (see Latour, 2005). Understanding systems impact requires using frameworks, terms, constructs, and categories that are capable of situating 4IR technologies within larger discussions of language and communication. In so doing, scholars and societies can better understand the very systems that facilitate and mediate life as we know it.

The need to establish a more robust empirical agenda based on language and technology should be evident in these three characteristics of 4IR. Technology is not only all around us, but it is embedded within the very systems that mediate how we think, behave, and communicate. The ability to navigate, as well as control, ongoing 4IR transformations is integral to a sustainable and equitable future that is inextricably connected to technology. Yet, technological changes are transforming life at such pace, reach, and matter that the disparity between what societies know and need to know is already great.

Previous sections have again identified numerous research topics that will help narrow this gap in knowledge. In addition to establishing an empirical agenda based on 4IR innovation and change, applied linguists can engage in innovative research-based practices that will help keep pace with ongoing technological transformations. These research practices are divided into three aspects of scholarship.

1. **Literacy**: Applied linguists can make greater contributions to scholarship on language and technology by developing literacies in current and emerging technologies. This learning process could entail better utilizing mobile applications to collect and manage data for research purposes, learning a coding language to understand the architecture of online spaces, and exploring how language is used in different modes of digital communication for personal and professional tasks, including classroom instruction, trading stocks, or finding a life partner, to name a few. The logic here is that proficiency in emerging technologies is essential to fully understanding how technological transformations are shaping language and communication. Literacy in such areas can be systematically developed by designing compulsory techno-literacy courses in applied linguistic programs at the undergraduate and graduate levels, creating more calls for special issues in journals that draw attention to 4IR transformations, and incentivizing applied linguists to study language and technology issues through grants and scholarships. Universities can also promote literacies in 4IR technologies by offering to pay for workshops that lead to professional technology-based certifications.

2. **Platform**: Applied linguists can make greater contributions to scholarship on language and technology by relying on different platforms to conduct research. Applied linguistic scholarship is overwhelmingly document-centric, using outdated and rigid platforms to publish and share research that does not reflect how many members of society consume news and information. Yet, 4IR transformations provide the means and spaces to publish and share information in different media and with diverse platforms. For example, applied linguists can utilize collaborative platforms to create "living" research papers that allow readers to provide constructive feedback or even make changes to a work-in-progress manuscript. VR worlds can be used to reimagine what it means to share research, allowing readers to communicate directly with authors either synchronously or asynchronously. Using a more diverse set of platforms to develop and share research findings would also help scholars reach a larger audience, including readers that do not have the means to pass through expensive publisher paywalls. Beyond these reasons to use more platforms to develop and share research findings, the future of applied linguistic scholarship is

dependent on the willingness and ability of researchers to conduct and disseminate research in ways that reflect how societies use technologies to create and consume information.

3. **Dissemination**: Applied linguists can make greater contributions to scholarship on language and technology by identifying and adopting concrete strategies to, for example, increase readership, reach a more diverse audience, and collaborate with technology professionals. These dissemination practices can be divided into three audience types: applied linguists, interdisciplinary scholars, and nonacademic professionals. An impactful way that applied linguists can directly contribute to technological change and innovation is to develop dissemination practices that speak directly to nonacademic professionals that are responsible for government policies, ethics guidelines, state funding, and technology designs. Applied linguistic scholarship can be used to speak directly to such professionals by reimagining what it means to conduct research in language and technology, designing empirical studies according to how nonacademics, such as government officials, institution leaders, and computer engineers, are accustomed to reading reports or receiving information. For instance, is it possible to disseminate research using shorter, conference proceedings that require less reading time as well as knowledge of applied linguistic jargon to understand the main findings of a study? Organizers of applied linguistic conferences, which are by and large mono-disciplinary in reach (Pennycook, 2018a), should consider teaming up with scholars working in cognate fields of study, such as researchers working in natural language processing or even computer science. Within applied linguistic circles, researchers can establish more open access journals that speak to different audience types, which requires the field to restructure performance metrics that determine what qualifies as a good publication.

This concise discussion of literacy, platform, and dissemination shows that contributions to 4IR knowledge generation is multifaceted, requiring efforts that include but transcend traditional forms of empirical research. Specifically, understanding 4IR transformations requires rethinking what knowledge is (Pennycook, 2018a), and how it can be used to engage in applied linguistic scholarship in an age of rapid technological change. Knowledge of this kind includes specialized training in software development or competences in information technology systems. Much like the foreign language requirement embedded in many applied linguistic and related programs, specialized training in technology should be considered in curricula discussions at higher education institutions as required or optional courses. It is indeed sensible to consider such curricula options given how much communication takes place in and through technology both for personal and professional purposes.

In addition, like most members of society, applied linguists are entangled in the very technologies that they seek to understand. Adopting a critical lens through which to understand such entanglements is necessary to step away from, and evaluate, the technologies that mediate the world that humans occupy. This lens need not come from the traditions that many associate with the word "critical," though such frameworks are needed to offer a complete picture of language and technology – see, for example, the writings of Fairclough, Wodak, and of course, van Dijk.

Indeed, these more traditional notions of what it means to apply a critical approach to language and discourse will play an increasingly important role in applied linguistic research: The task of reflecting on, making sense of, and adjusting to, the many pressing social and linguistic issues facing societies requires a theoretical apparatus that is capable of untangling its complex web of meaning (to which critical discourse analysts have devoted their field). For instance, scholarship has uncovered salient issues ranging from technology and social media (e.g., Rambe, 2012) to pedagogy and classroom discourse (e.g., Jenks, 2020). Critical applied linguistic research creates opportunities to reflect on the power dynamics embedded within societies, and in some cases, address issues of power in transformational discourses and outcomes. Accordingly, critical approaches and perspectives in applied linguistics are well-placed to understand systems of power entangled in 4IR transformations, as language and communication are central to how systemic inequalities, social hierarchies, and cultural dynamics are enforced within societies. For example, Brock (2018) uses critical discourse analysis as a springboard to understand how culture is produced and reproduced in and through ideology and technological practice as a clearly identifiable genre of communication. In Brock's (2018) data set, "Black Twitter" is used to demonstrate how socially fabricated constructs, such as race, are embedded within, but also persistently influenced by, technology.

Another critical lens may take the perspective of what ethnomethodologists call "member" knowledge or "membership knowledge." For ethnomethodologists, member knowledge refers to the understanding that one develops through participation in, or membership of, a community of practice, such as working in an office, driving a delivery truck, or playing an online, multiplayer game. An ethnomethodological understanding of member knowledge is not merely an acknowledgement of the empirical value in knowing the people and practices being investigated. Member knowledge is a topic of discussion and investigation for ethnomethodologists (Ten Have, 2005). For language and technology studies, an ethnomethodological understanding of member knowledge may consist of mastering the competencies needed to design or manage a technological device or application, which provides the foundation to either conduct research of the kind discussed in this Element or directly take part in the advancement of such technologies (for an older, but interesting take on how ethnomethodology can be used in information system, see Crabtree, 2003).

Indeed, applied linguistic scholarship has a long and rich tradition of possessing the competences to understand the practices of the participants under investigation and the ability to identify solutions to improve the context to which such practices are applied. For instance, many applied linguistic scholars spend many years if not decades teaching in the very contexts that represent their focus of investigation. Furthermore, a defining characteristic of applied linguistic scholarship is the investigation of languages that are second or additional to the L1s of the researchers: The backstory is of course that applied linguists devote their lives mastering the different languages used by (or which happen to represent) their research participants.

Member knowledge is thus a familiar resource used in applied linguistic scholarship, yet one that can be exploited in transformative and paradigmatic ways, as highlighted earlier in the discussion of three research practices: literacy, platform, and dissemination. Of course, a broader discussion of how applied linguists can transform the member knowledge of 4IR technologies into empirical research is needed, which begins both internally within the field and externally amongst researchers working in other academic disciplines.

However, calls to incorporate more technology into research and teaching must contend with the contrarian view that 4IR transformations are neither presently upon us nor influencing in any significant way how societies function. To this argument, it is necessary to revisit the position(s) of technological determinism.

Technological determinism is the belief that societies at multiple levels of human sociality and in various domains of life are experiencing significant changes because of technology. Many versions of technological determinism exist. The strong version suggests that humans have little to no control over technologies or that technologies are nearly or completely autonomous. Weaker versions stress the importance of treating technologies as distinct contexts that present users with different affordances and constraints.

An alternative paradigm to technological determinism exists, which stresses the importance of human agency. This paradigm is referred to as the social construction of technology.

Social construction of technology is the belief that technology is a social construct. That is, technology exists within contexts of human sociality. More specifically, technology exists because of humans, and their desires to accomplish different social or communicative goals (see Pinch & Bijker, 1984). Like the weaker versions of technological determinism, proponents of the social construction of technology stress the importance of context, highlighting the intimate relationship between the design and use of technologies on the one hand; and on the other hand, the social, as well as cultural, particularities that shape how such technologies come to existence.

Technological determinism and the social construction of technology offer competing frameworks for investigating language and technology issues, but this does not mean that researchers must actively engage in such theoretical debates. While it is important to locate future applied linguistic research within a theoretical framework, there are other frameworks that can be used to carve out an empirical agenda in language and technology studies.

For example, posthumanism is a particularly useful theoretical construct that adds to existing discussions of technological determinism and the social construction of technology. Although posthumanism was identified and discussed in Section 2, it is important to discuss how this theoretical construct fits within larger disciplinary and paradigmatic concerns.

Posthumanism is again the position that an anthropocentric view of sociality is misguided in a world that has experienced significant ecological damage because of human negligence. Proponents of posthumanism possess a range of diverging beliefs, but most scholars are of the view that humans are part of a larger ecosystem of physical, material, digital, and technological connections that must be attended to when reflecting on, and making decisions related to, human sociality.

Posthumanism can offer applied linguists an optimistic take on the human potential in that one school of thought imagines a "post-human" world that pushes the physical and psychological boundaries of mankind by harnessing the power of technology (for a discussion of posthumanism and higher education, see Gourlay, 2020). A posthuman world that uses technology to enhance human cognitive abilities, such as memory retention and capacity, is one such example. Future research within this view of posthumanism must begin with a rejection of the human-machine binary, instead considering the two as inseparable and indispensable to one another. Applied linguistic scholarship can adopt this more optimistic view of humans and machines, building on the excellent work that has already been done using (and based on) technology: for example, existing work has looked at empirical topics ranging from mobility studies and mediated discourse (McIlvenny, 2019) to eye tracking research and memory tests (Conklin, Pellicer-Sánchez, & Carrol, 2018). Some work has also started to look at areas of study within applied linguistics through the lens of posthumanism (e.g., O'Halloran, 2022).

The more mainstream position within posthumanism, however, places humans outside of discussions of technology, seeking empirical answers that are not weighed down by the human experience (Pennycook, 2017). In this sense, the mainstream posthumanism (Wolfe, 2010) view relies on the human-machine binary, and more specifically, is inherently critical of what human subjectivities can offer discussions of language and technology. This more pessimistic view may entail research that sees emergent technologies as socially problematic and an outcome of decades of societal decisions that ignore the ecology to which humans belong. Many empirical topics that are based on the human-machine binary can be investigated (e.g., Pennycook, 2018b), starting from the more general position that designates humans as the catalysts to, and reasons for, the problems that exist in society, such as online mental health among adolescents and teenagers (e.g., Verduyn et al., 2017).

The tendency within posthumanism to reject the human experience as the primary or sole lens through which to understand language and technology is on the surface an appropriate position to take given the role humans have played in past and current environmental and social disasters. However, it could also be said that human subjectivities are needed now more than ever to confront the social issues that 4IR transformations bring to the world. For example, establishing greater financial and social value in the Humanities can help provide alternative and competing narratives to discourses, which often come from Big Tech and related academic fields, that unequivocally support the idea that emergent technologies are not a threat to mankind and that human agency is not lost in societies tied to 4IR transformations.

As noted in the previous section, human agency is a central issue in future research on language and technology. Applied linguists can add to existing work in the area by examining how individuals understand, and what they feel about, human agency. While this more traditional applied linguistic topic is not innovative in a technological sense, ideologies are an important aspect of capturing the relationship between humans and machines. That is, belief systems can help researchers understand how societies conceptualize and operationalize their relationship with, and dependency on, technologies. Human agency could also be examined by looking at existing situations where 4IR transformations have already replaced humans at work, such as in the service industry and manufacturing. Investigating what humans think about such contexts, as well as their interactions with autonomous technologies, will help future research attend to important societal issues ranging from state policies on worker protection to the coordination of embodied movements between humans and machines. Of course, applied linguists can investigate their own workplace practices, reflecting on the ways in which AI tools are used to facilitate or replace empirical activities traditionally done by humans (e.g., transcribing, organizing, and analyzing data).

The use of AI in research is a fitting way to end a discussion of the contributions applied linguistic scholarship can make to future language and technology studies. Walch (2019), in her short but highly influential editorial piece on AI, summarizes the importance of 4IR transformations in seven patterns of innovation: hyperpersonalization, autonomous systems, predictive analytics and decision support, conversational/human interactions, patterns and anomalies, recognition systems, and goal-driven systems. Although not an "academic" paper in the traditional sense of the term, Walch's (2019) work is not only impactful both in and outside of academic circles, her seven patterns of AI are also relevant to a discussion of what applied linguists can do in the future to make greater contributions to language and technology studies. These seven patterns of AI innovation also offer a different way of summarizing the issues, themes, and empirical topics discussed throughout this Element.

1. **Hyperpersonalization** is the use of AI in general, and machine learning in particular, to gather information from individuals with the goal of streamlining their tasks and responsibilities, such as curating online content (e.g., YouTube) or recommending services and products (e.g., Google Ads). Hyperpersonalization requires gathering, tracking, storing, and processing user information, and thus there are many ethical issues that can be investigated from an applied linguistic perspective, as discussed in previous sections and most notably in Section 4. Research into hyperpersonalization is relevant to language and technology studies, as issues of privacy, consent, freedom, and free will are discursively expressed at multiple levels of society from anonymous online forum discussions to public policy debates between opposing political parties.

2. **Autonomous systems** are devices and applications that operate without, or with minimal, human support after the initial design and implementation phase. Autonomous systems are software or hardware designs that possess specific responsibilities, such as tracking user behavior on a website, sorting through parts on an assembly line, or navigating a vehicle down a busy road. Autonomous systems are relevant to language and technology studies in several ways: Themes that applied linguists can investigate within autonomous systems include, but are not limited to, the communicative capabilities

of, and the interactions that stem from, machines and robots. Much has already been said about the specific issues and topics that can be investigated here, as discussed in Section 2.

3. **Predictive analytics and decision support** refer to the common practice of making conclusions based on information gathered by AI systems. The information needed to make decisions that are increasingly more precise or accurate are historical records of human behavior and current user data. Predictive analytics and decision support are widely used because there is an assumption within most societies that for many tasks machines can make more informed and better decisions than humans. Systems that rely on predictive analytics are relevant to language and technology studies in a number of ways: One area that has received very little empirical attention is in predictive texts (e.g., autocorrection and word suggestions), and the ways in which input systems mediate language and communication (Arnold, Chauncey, & Gajos, 2020). Future researchers may wish to look at how writers make stylistic or structural decisions according to AI-based information or examine the ways in which mobile texting is transformed when predictive texts are enabled.

4. **Conversational/human interactions** is the category of AI that encompasses all of the communicative encounters that involve a machine. Such encounters include communicating to, as well as with, machines. As discussed in Section 2, AI communication can also be categorized into four modes of communication: human-machine-human, human-machine, machine-human, machine-machine. Within these four modes of communication, applied linguists can study many empirical issues, such as how keyboards, screens, microphones, headphones shape register, turn-taking, and word choice; or the ways in which virtual assistants and robots mediate conversational structure and topic management. Conversations and human interactions based on AI technologies are key areas of applied linguistic research, as the evolution of AI conversations is contingent upon understanding the mediation between machines and language.

5. **Patterns and anomalies** are AI systems that, in the same processes involved in predictive analytics and decision support, help humans make decisions based on information gathered from historical and current user data. Notable industries that use AI systems to identify patterns and anomalies include banking and security. In such industries, detecting fraud, calculation errors, security breaches, and vulnerabilities in the context of big data (e.g., unfathomable amounts of information on user behaviors) requires placing significant trust into machines and relinquishing some human agency. Although initial research suggests that individuals are aware and manage issues of

online privacy and protection to varying degrees of efficacy (Boerman, Kruikemeier, & Zuiderveen Borgesius, 2021), there are many ethical and moral questions that linger. As discussed in Section 4, reliance on AI tools that are capable of detecting patterns and anomalies is necessary given the amount of information required to make informed decisions on, for example, banking or security. An important topic to investigate by applied linguists includes the ways in which powerful institutions, such as state governments or Big Tech companies, discursively construct notions of privacy and rights in discussions of what is good for societies (see Section 5).

6. **Recognition systems** are devices and applications that are designed to tease out information from a larger set of data. In streaming or recorded videos, for instance, recognitions systems built on AI technologies (e.g., machines and deep learning) are capable of identifying and categorizing specific objects (e.g., people and bags at an airport) or movements (e.g., the body posture and gestures embodied during a meeting) based on preprogrammed criteria. Recognitions systems can also process facial features (e.g., facial recognition on phones), sounds (e.g., dictation software), as well as texts (e.g., texting using predictive language), to name a few. In news media, much is said about the use of recognition systems by institutions and governments to complete tasks and fulfill responsibilities once managed by humans, as well as the ethical and moral issues that come with relying on such technologies (Hagendorff, 2020). Sections 4 and 5 have identified a number of related empirical issues that can be investigated, including most notably the five categories of 4IR threats: rights, information, control, representation, and security.

7. **Goal-driven systems** are applications that are able to make "autonomous" decisions while in operation according to preprogrammed information. Familiar examples of goal-driven systems are gaming applications that allow humans to compete against machines, such as in chess. Using pro-grammed information, goal-driven systems can "learn" how to accomplish particular goals, responding on the fly to different input, such as the strategic moves made on a board by a highly skilled human chess player. More practical examples of goal-driven systems include planning, navigating, and problem-solving. An interesting area of investigation is in the coordin-ation of human movement and communication within spatial environments mediated by goal-driven systems, such as in pedestrian traffic lights (see, for example, Merlino & Mondada, 2019).

AI technologies are following a sharp upward evolutionary trajectory that will continue to significantly influence how societies operate, as encapsulated in the seven patterns of innovation. The use of AI, as well as other 4IR technologies, in many domains of life is a reminder of the need to investigate language and technology in greater detail and with more concerted effort in future applied linguistic research. As discussed in this Element on several occasions, there is a real danger in not identifying, tracking, and investigating such innovation and change, as technology is progressing at a rate that is making it increasingly more difficult to comprehend. Yet, applied linguistic scholarship is well-placed to investigate the mediation between 4IR technologies and language, as the field has a long tradition of investigating the ways in which societies use and make sense of languages.

The empirical potential in research on language and technology is best summarized by returning to, and ending with, the radical changes that are occurring as a result of 4IR technologies. Like previous industrial revolutions, 4IR innovation and change are so pervasive that everything from an individual's sense of identity and understanding of the world to the economic success of an entire industry (and indeed country) are crucially dependent on its technological systems. Although applied linguists are in an excellent position to contribute to language and technology scholarship, interdisciplinary research with societal impact is needed now more than ever. This Element has identified numerous empirical issues and themes that applied linguists can investigate in the pursuit of interdisciplinary and impactful research. In addition to researching such issues and themes, this Element explored how 4IR technologies can be harnessed to more efficiently publish and disseminate timely research. This Element has also offered an overview of what can and needs to be done in future research, arguing that applied linguistics are in a privileged position to move language and technology studies forward.

References

Agency for Healthcare Research and Quality. (2021). *Poverty and Access to Internet, by County: Social Determinants of Health*. Social Determinants of Health Database. https://apastyle.apa.org/style-grammar-guidelines/refer ences/examples/report-government-agency-references.

Alao, O. D., Joshua, J. V., & Akinsola, J. E. T. (2019). Human computer interaction (HCI) and smart home applications. *IUP Journal of Information Technology*, 15(3), 7–21.

Andersson, M. (2021). The climate of climate change: Impoliteness as a hallmark of homophily in YouTube comment threads on Greta Thunberg's environmental activism. *Journal of Pragmatics*, 178, 93–107.

Andrée, B. P. J., Chamorro, A., Spencer, P., Koomen, E., & Dogo, H. (2019). Revisiting the relation between economic growth and the environment; a global assessment of deforestation, pollution and carbon emission. *Renewable and Sustainable Energy Reviews*, 114, 109221. www.sciencedirect .com/science/article/pii/S1364032119304216.

Andujar, A., & Buchner, J. (2019). The potential of 3D virtual reality (VR) for language learning: An overview. In *Proceedings of the 15th International Conference Mobile Learning* (pp. 153–156). Utrecht.

Araujo, T., Helberger, N., Kruikemeier, S., & De Vreese, C. H. (2020). In AI we trust? Perceptions about automated decision-making by artificial intelligence. *AI & SOCIETY*, 35(3), 611–623.

Arnold, K. C., Chauncey, K., & Gajos, K. Z. (2020). Predictive text encourages predictable writing. March. In *Proceedings of the 25th International Conference on Intelligent User Interfaces* (pp. 128–138). New York, NY.

Atala, A., & Yoo, J. J. (2015). *Essentials of 3D Biofabrication and Translation*. New York: Academic Press.

Baldwin, J. (2018). In digital we trust: Bitcoin discourse, digital currencies, and decentralized network fetishism. *Palgrave Communications*, 4(1), 1–10.

Barad, K. (2007). *Meeting the Universe Halfway: Quantum Physics and the Entanglement of Matter and Meaning*. Durham, NC: Duke University Press.

Barnard-Wills, D. (2012). *Surveillance and Identity: Discourse, Subjectivity and the State*. Surrey: Ashgate.

Barracuda. (2021). *Bot Attacks: Top Threats and Trends*. Volume 1. September. www.barracuda.com/bot-threat-report.

Bhatia, A., & Jenks, C. J. (2018). Fabricating the American dream in US media portrays of Syrian refugees: A discourse analytical study. *Discourser & Communication*, 12(3), 221–239.

Bhatia, V. K., Candlin, C. N., & Engberg, J. (2008). *Legal Discourse across Cultures and Systems*. Hong Kong: Hong Kong University Press.

Block, D. (2013). *Social Class in Applied Linguistics*. London: Routledge.

Block, D., Gray, J., & Holborow, M. (2012). *Neoliberalism and Applied Linguistics*. London: Routledge.

Boerman, S. C., Kruikemeier, S., & Zuiderveen Borgesius, F. J. (2021). Exploring motivations for online privacy protection behavior: Insights from panel data. *Communication Research*, 48(7), 953–977.

Bonarini, A. (2020). Communication in human-robot interaction. *Current Robotics Reports*, 1, 279–285.

Brock, A. (2018). Critical technocultural discourse analysis. *New Media & Society*, 20(3), 1012–1030.

Brumfit, C. J. (1995). Teacher professionalism and research. In G. Cook & B. Seidlhofer (Eds.), *Principle and Practice in Applied Linguistics* (pp. 27–41). Oxford: Oxford University Press.

Cap, P. (2017). *The Language of Fear: Communicating Threat in Public Discourse*. London: Palgrave Macmillan.

Chohan, U. W. (2021). *Counter-Hegemonic Finance: The Gamestop Short Squeeze*. http://dx.doi.org/10.2139/ssrn.3775127.

Cronin, M. (1998). The cracked looking glass of servants: Translation and minority languages in a global age. *The Translator*, 4(2), 145–162.

Crabtree, A. (2003). Taking technomethodology seriously: Hybrid change in the ethnomethodology–design relationship. *European Journal of Information Systems*, 13(3), 195–209.

Conklin, K., Pellicer-Sánchez, A., & Carrol, G. (2018). *Eye-Tracking: A Guide for Applied Linguistics Research*. Cambridge: Cambridge University Press.

Curran, N. M. (2020). Intersectional English(es) and the gig economy: Teaching English online. *International Journal of Communication*, 14, 2667–2686.

Curran, N. M. (2021). Discrimination in the gig economy: The experiences of Black online English teachers. *Language and Education*, 37(3), 1–15.

van Dijk, T. (1993). *Elite Discourse and Racism*. London: Sage.

Dodigovic, M. (2005). *Artificial Intelligence in Second Language Learning: Raising Error Awareness*. Bristol: Multilingual Matters.

Due, B. L, & Toft,T. (2021). Phygital highlighting: Achieving joint visual attention when physically co-editing a digital text. *Journal of Pragmatics*, 177, 1–17.

Eggers, D. (2014). *The Circle*. New York: Vintage Books.

European Commission. (2022). *Towards a Green, Digital and Resilient Economy: Our European Growth Model*. Brussels: Communication from the Commission to the European Parliament, the European Council, the European Economic and Social Committee and the Committee of the Regions.

Federal Bureau of Investigation (2020). *Internet Crime Report 2020*.

Feng, W., & Ren, W. (2020). Impoliteness in negative online consumer reviews: A cross- language and cross-sector comparison. *Intercultural Pragmatics*, 17(1), 1–25.

Flaxman, S., Goel, S., & Rao, J. M. (2016). Filter bubbles, echo chambers, and online news consumption. *Public Opinion Quarterly*, 80(S1), 298–320.

Gamble, C. N., Hanan, J. S., & Nail, T. (2019). What is new materialism? *Angelaki*, 24(6), 111–134.

Georgalou, M. (2016). "I make the rules on my Wall": Privacy and identity management practices on Facebook. *Discourse & Communication*, 10(1), 40–64.

Gourlay, L. (2020). *Posthumanism and the Digital University: Texts, Bodies and Materialities*. London: Bloomsbury.

Graham, M. (2019). *Digital Economies at Global Margins*. Cambridge, MA: MIT Press.

Grudin, J., & Jacques, R. (2019). Chatbots, humbots, and the quest for artificial general intelligence. May. *Proceedings of the 2019 CHI Conference on Human Factors in Computing Systems* (pp. 1–11). Glasgow.

Guinchard, A. (2021). Our digital footprint under Covid-19: Should we fear the UK digital contact tracing app? *International Review of Law, Computers & Technology*, 35(1), 84–97.

Haff, P. (2014). Humans and technology in the Anthropocene: Six rules. *The Anthropocene Review*, 1(2), 126–136.

Hagendorff, T. (2020). The ethics of AI ethics: An evaluation of guidelines. *Minds and Machines*, 30(1), 99–120.

Hancock, J. T., Naaman, M., & Levy, K. (2020). AI-mediated communication: Definition, research agenda, and ethical considerations. *Journal of Computer-Mediated Communication*, 25(1), 89–100.

Hemphill, T. A. (2002). Electronic commerce and consumer privacy: Establishing online trust in the US digital economy. *Business and Society Review*, 107(2), 221–239.

Iivari, N., Kinnula, M., Molin-Juustila, T., & Kuure, L. (2016). Exclusions in social inclusion projects: Struggles in involving children in digital technology development. *Info Systems*, 28, 1020–1048.

Jenks, C. J. (2020). Applying critical discourse analysis to classrooms. *Classroom Discourse*, 11(2), 99–106.

Jordan, M. I., & Mitchell, T. M. (2015). Machine learning: Trends, perspectives, and prospects. *Science*, 349(6245), 255–260.

Kellogg, K. C., Valentine, M. A., & Christin, A. (2020). Algorithms at work: The new contested terrain of control. *Academy of Management Annals*, 14(1), 366–410.

Latour, B. (2005). *Reassembling the Social: An Introduction to Actor-Network-Theory*. Oxford: Oxford University Press.

Lock, S. (2021). "Not great news": US boss fires 900 employees on a Zoom call. *The Guardian*. December 7. www.theguardian.com/us-news/2021/dec/07/not-great-news-us-boss-fires-900-employees-on-a-zoom-call.

Master, F. (2021). Meet Grace, the healthcare robot COVID-19 created. *Reuters*. June 9. www.reuters.com/business/healthcare-pharmaceuticals/meet-grace-healthcare-robot-covid-19-created-2021–06–09/.

McIlvenny, P. (2019). "It's going to be very slippery": Snow, space and mobility while learning cross-country skiing. In O. B. Jensen, C. Lassen & I. S. G. Lange (Eds.), *Material Mobilities* (pp. 77–100). London: Routledge.

Merlino, S., & Mondada, L. (2019). Crossing the street: How pedestrians interact with cars. *Language & Communication*, 65, 131–147.

Mulligan, C. (2018). Blockchain and sustainable growth. *United Nations: UN Chronicle*, LV(3&4). December. www.un.org/en/un-chronicle/blockchain-and-sustainable-growth.

Narayanan, A., Bonneau, J., Felten, E., Miller, A., & Goldfeder, S. (2016). *Bitcoin and Cryptocurrency Technologies: A Comprehensive Introduction*. Princeton, NJ: Princeton University Press.

O'Halloran, K. (2022). Posthumanism and corpus linguistics. In A. O'Keeffe & M.J. McCarthy (Eds.), *The Routledge Handbook of Corpus Linguistics* (pp. 675–692). London: Routledge.

Pennycook, A. (2017). *Posthumanist Applied Linguistics*. London: Routledge.

Pennycook, A. (2018a). Applied linguistics as epistemic assemblage. *AILA Review*, 31, 113–134.

Pennycook, A. (2018b). Posthumanist applied linguistics. *Applied Linguistics*, 39(4), 445–461.

Pilkington, M. (2016). Blockchain technology: Principles and applications. In F. Xavier Olleros & M. Zhegu (Eds.), *Research Handbook on Digital Transformations* (pp. 225–253). Cheltenham: Edward Elgar.

Pinch, T. J., & Bijker, W. E. (1984). The social construction of facts and artefacts: Or how the sociology of science and the sociology of technology might benefit each other. *Social Studies of Science*, 14(3), 399–441.

Rambe, P. (2012). Critical discourse analysis of collaborative engagement in Facebook postings. *Australasian Journal of Educational Technology*, 28(2). https://doi.org/10.14742/ajet.875.

Ricento, T. (Ed.). (2015). *Language Policy and Political Economy: English in a Global Context*. Oxford: Oxford University Press.

Risse, M. (2018). Human rights and artificial intelligence: An urgently needed agenda. *Human Rights Quarterly*, 41, 1–17.

Rosentiel, T. (2012). *State of the news media 2012*. Pew Research Center. www .pewresearch.org/2012/03/19/state-of-the-news-media–2012/.

Schwab, K. (2016). *The Fourth Industrial Revolution*. London: Portfolio Penguin.

Schwab, K. (2018). *Shaping the Future of the Fourth Industrial Revolution*. New York: Currency.

Shilton, K., & Greene, D. (2019). Linking platforms, practices, and developer ethics: Levers for privacy discourse in mobile application development. *Journal of Business Ethics*, 155(1), 131–146.

Silverman, C., Timberg, C., Kao, J., & Merrill, J. B. (2022). Facebook hosted surge of misinformation and insurrection threats in months leading up to Jan. 6 attack, records show. *Propublica*. www.propublica.org/article/face book-hosted-surge-of-misinformation-and-insurrection-threats-in-months-leading-up-to-jan-6-attack-records-show.

Sismondo, S. (2009). *An Introduction to Science and Technology Studies*. Oxford: Wiley-Blackwell.

Ten Have, P. (2005). The notion of member is the heart of the matter: On the role of membership knowledge in ethnomethodological inquiry. *Historical Social Research*, 30(1), 28–53.

Thomas, D. (2020). *Cybercrime Losses: An eExamination of U.S. Manufacturing and the Totaleconomy*. Advanced Manufacturing Series (NIST AMS), National Institute of Standards and Technology. https://doi .org/10.6028/NIST.AMS.100-32.

Varis, P. (2019). Conspiracy theorising online: Memes as a conspiracy theory genre. *Tilburg Papers in Culture Studies* No. 238. chrome-extension:// efaidnbmnnnibpcajpcglclefindmkaj/https://www.tilburguniversity.edu/sites/ default/files/download/TPCS_238-Varis.pdf.

Verduyn, P., Ybarra, O., Résibois, M., Jonides, J., & Kross, E. (2017). Do social network sites enhance or undermine subjective well-being? A critical review. *Social Issues and Policy Review*, 11(1), 274–302.

Vincent, J. (2022). Meta announces plans to build an AI-powered "universal speech translator." *The Verge*. February 23. www.theverge.com/2022/2/23/ 22947368/meta-facebook-ai-universal-speech-translation-project.

Walch, K. (2019). The seven patterns of AI. *Forbes.* www.forbes.com/sites/cognitiveworld/2019/09/17/the-seven-patterns-of-ai/?sh=599ccdaf12d0.

Wang, S. (2021). Consumers beware: How are your favorite "free" investment apps regulated? *Duke Law & Technology Review*, 19, 43–58.

Weizenbaum, J. (1966). ELIZA—A computer program for the study of natural language communication between man and machine. *Computational Linguistics*, 9(1), 36–45.

West, D. W. (2015). *Digital Divide: Improving Internet Access in the Developing World through Affordable Services and Diverse Content.* The Brookings Institute. www.brookings.edu/wp-content/uploads/2016/06/West_Internet-Access.pdf.

Williams, H. T., McMurray, J. R., Kurz, T., & Lambert, F. H. (2015). Network analysis reveals open forums and echo chambers in social media discussions of climate change. *Global Environmental Change*, 32, 126–138.

Wolfe, C. (2010). *What is Posthumanism?* Minneapolis, MN: University of Minnesota.

Yin, R., Wang, D., Zhao, S., Lou, Z., & Shen, G. (2021). Wearable sensors-enabled human–machine interaction systems: From design to application. *Advanced Functional Materials*, 31(11), 2008936. https://onlinelibrary.wiley.com/doi/10.1002/adfm.202008936.

Young, H. (2015). The digital language divide. *Guardian.* http://labs.theguardian.com/digital-language-divide/.

Zúñiga, H., Copeland, L., & Bimber, B. (2013). Political consumerism: Civic engagement and the social media connection. *New Media & Society*, 16(3), 488–506.

Cambridge Elements ☰

Applied Linguistics

Li Wei
University College London

Li Wei is Chair of Applied Linguistics at the UCL Institute of Education, University College London (UCL), and Fellow of Academy of Social Sciences, UK. His research covers different aspects of bilingualism and multilingualism. He was the founding editor of the following journals: *International Journal of Bilingualism* (Sage), *Applied Linguistics Review* (De Gruyter), *Language, Culture and Society* (Benjamins), *Chinese Language and Discourse* (Benjamins) and *Global Chinese* (De Gruyter), and is currently Editor of the *International Journal of Bilingual Education and Bilingualism* (Taylor and Francis). His books include the *Blackwell Guide to Research Methods in Bilingualism and Multilingualism* (with Melissa Moyer) and *Translanguaging: Language, Bilingualism and Education* (with Ofelia Garcia) which won the British Association of Applied Linguistics Book Prize.

Zhu Hua
University College London

Zhu Hua is Professor of Language Learning and Intercultural Communication at the UCL Institute of Education, University College London (UCL) and is a Fellow of Academy of Social Sciences, UK. Her research is centred around multilingual and intercultural communication. She has also studied child language development and language learning. She is book series co-editor for *Routledge Studies in Language and Intercultural Communication* and *Cambridge Key Topics in Applied Linguistics*, and Forum and Book Reviews Editor of *Applied Linguistics* (Oxford University Press).

About the Series

Mirroring the *Cambridge Key Topics in Applied Linguistics*, this Elements series focuses on the key topics, concepts and methods in Applied Linguistics today. It revisits core conceptual and methodological issues in different subareas of Applied Linguistics. It also explores new emerging themes and topics. All topics are examined in connection with real-world issues and the broader political, economic and ideological contexts.

Cambridge Elements ≡

Applied Linguistics

Elements in the Series

Viral Discourse
Edited by Rodney H. Jones

Second Language Pragmatics
Wei Ren

Kongish: Translanguaging and the Commodification of an Urban Dialect
Tong King Lee

Metalinguistic Awareness in Second Language Reading Development
Sihui Echo Ke, Dongbo Zhang and Keiko Koda

Crisis Leadership: Boris Johnson and Political Persuasion during the Covid Pandemic
Philip Seargeant

Writing Banal Inequalities: How to Fabricate Stories Which Disrupt
Edited by Hannah Cowan and Alfonso Del Percio

New Frontiers in Language and Technology
Christopher Joseph Jenks

A full series listing is available at www.cambridge.org/EIAL

Printed in the United States
by Baker & Taylor Publisher Services